A Prisoner's Fight

Written by:
Nicholas Chittick

Cadmus Publishing
www.cadmuspublishing.com

AUTHOR'S NOTE

Contrary to what my mother insisted while she was still alive, I'm not special. Mine is only one of many thousands of accounts on how the pandemic affected the men and women inside America's jails and prisons. My story probably isn't even the most interesting. I will say this, though; no matter who you are or where you were, the year 2020 totally sucked. That's just facts. No matter how bad you feel you had it out there in the free world, however, please allow me to assure you with the utmost sincerity that it was far less enjoyable to endure COVID-19 as a guest of a correctional facility, especially inside the Illinois Department of Corrections.

Before we get started, I suppose I ought to give you a bit of backstory on my life, such as it is, leading up to the pandemic. A little context. So, buckle up, because HERE…WE…GO!

DEDICATION PAGE

For Cathy

FOREWORD

This is a book about real places, people, and events. As for the events, I've done my best to describe them without embellishment. Each occurrence is described how it happened as I recall it. I've also done my best to maintain chronological integrity. I reconstructed the timeline based on my own human memory, so if there are any errors, they are solely my own. As to the places and people written of herein, I've done my best to represent them accurately. Interactions are described exactly as I remember them. Words ascribed to individuals are written exactly as I remember them being spoken.

If anyone feels misrepresented, I sincerely apologize. I tried to be as accurate as possible, and I sincerely hope that I've honestly represented what the prisoners of the Illinois Department of Corrections had to endure during the pandemic. Every so often the media will interview a prison inmate. Usually, we prisoners are not impressed with this person that "they" have chosen as our spokesperson. We will say to ourselves in unison, "Why did they put THIS clown on TV?"

Yeah, I don't want to be that guy. I hope I got it right.

CONTENTS

CHAPTER ONE

Pre-Pandemic

Full disclosure, right from the start, I'm a minority; a white guy in prison. I'm also full of contradictions, as I believe most people are. I'm Christian, but cuss like a drunken fucking sailor. I don't like white, nationalist conservatives or self-righteous, overreacting liberals. I think they're both equally bad for America. I have known, and currently know, many African American and Latino men and women whom I consider brothers and sisters, yet I'll laugh at a racist joke. What do you call a black man hitchhiking in Utah? Stranded! C'mon, it's funny. I believe in the Second Amendment, and I fully support a woman's right to choose. My point is that nothing in my life is cut and dry. I have this perpetual inner struggle going on within me. What I should do, I don't, and what I shouldn't do, I do, because my carnal nature is at constant war with my spirit. My spirit is willing, but the flesh is weak, and that is true of anyone who is alive. I told you, I'm not special.

I'm in prison for murder. Nothing particularly noteworthy, not serial killing or mafia hits. Just a drug deal gone bad. I caught my case in 1998 and had no criminal history prior to that. No need to sugar coat it; I was a crackhead. I could say I had a serious drug dependency problem, but nope. Let's keep it real. Crackhead.

After two-and-a-half years in notorious Cook County Jail the prosecutor in my case offered me 20 years to plead guilty, so I did. I took the deal. I was, in fact, guilty, and the state was, in fact, seeking the death penalty. Twenty years seemed like a win. Well…maybe not a win, but better than the alternative.

But the judge pulled a fast one on me at my sentencing hearing. Didn't give me the 20, gave me 28 instead, no backsies. This isn't unusual, it happens in Cook County, Illinois all the time. My mistake was not getting the deal in writing. Always get it in writing.

My sentencing hearing was in March of 2001. After my sentencing I went back to my cell and stared into the murky, stainless-steel mirror. I blinked a couple times, then when I looked up it was 2018.

Okay, maybe it didn't happen quite like that, but it is amazing how time passes in prison. Decades slip by almost without notice, sort of how a large ship can travel vast distances on the open sea without seeming to go anywhere. On the ocean there are no landmarks against which to measure your progress. Thousands of miles can pass with only the same unchanging view day after day. Years in prison are much the same as miles on the ocean.

January of 2018 found me arriving at a new prison--Graham Correctional Center in Hillsboro, Illinois. If you happen to be a UFC fan, Hillsboro is the hometown of Matt Hughes. Graham was my sixth correctional facility and twentieth year of incarceration. Each successive prison I'd transferred to through the years was a step down security-wise and represented a marked increase in privileges and programs. Graham was my first medium security facility.

I'd been in Cook County Jail's Division 11 (supermax), Joliet (max), Menard (max), Galesburg (medium-max), Danville (medium-max), and Graham (medium). Graham was the best prison that I'd ever been in up to that point, with TWO important discrepancies.

I'm a lifelong musician and guitarist. I say lifelong because according to my mother, when I was very young, I had a xylophone I used to play with. One of the little toy ones with the different colored tin bars you hit with a small plastic mallet. She insists that even before I learned to speak I would strike the instrument, much to her amazement, in repeating patterns and phrases instead of randomly banging on it like a normal kid, though she conceded that I also did that too sometimes. By the time I was ten I could read music, play clarinet, and I was pretty good on guitar. Pretty good for an adult. For a 10-year-old kid I was off the charts.

Anyway, back on topic. Danville Correctional Center is where I spent 2011 through 2018. Without question, hands down, they had the best band program in the entire Illinois Department of Corrections. I was there throughout the tenure of four different LTS (that's Leisure Time Services) Supervisors, each of whom let me have free run of the band room. I loved it, because when I'm playing music, I'm free. If not for what happened I'd have never left, I'd still be there today. What happened, you ask?

Okay, another digression. It'll be quick, I promise. I normally don't like talking about this, but I'll make an exception for you, dear reader. Just this once. Keep this on the down low.

One of the many job assignments I held at Danville was working in the gym. One day while in the gym going about my daily responsibilities, my attention was drawn to two African American gentlemen on the basketball court who'd suddenly found themselves engaged in a spirited contest of fisticuffs. One of the gents did not fare so well; he got the livin' shit beat out of him. Not the living, but the livin'. His opponent put it on him something decent. Long story short, the next day Internal Affairs called me over to their office, sat me down, and asked, "Who was fighting?"

I, of course, say, "Fight? What fight?" They say, "Chittick, we know there was a fight, and we know you cleaned up the blood and gave the loser a bunch of paper towels to clean himself up so he could make it back to the cellhouse without getting caught."

Man, that's what's wrong with prison these days. Too much snitching. Why'd they have to put me in it? What'd I do? If I'd been thinking on my feet I'd have played the white-boy card, said "Beats me, couple of black guys, they all look alike to me." But that's not how things went down. I stuck to my story, playing dumb, and they didn't buy it. They red-flagged me; no more band, no more job, no more anything. IA told me I'd never have another job or privilege again in that prison. They even kicked me out of DanVets, a rehabilitation program for incarcerated military veterans, like I wasn't a veteran anymore. It was time to go. That's why I left Danville for Graham.

So, the first discrepancy in Graham's position as "best prison" was that they didn't have a band program, sadly. They actually used to back in the day, but they converted the rooms allocated for prisoner band and art programs to use as storage for officer shh…stuff. Tactical gear and other unnecessary bullsh…things. But they had a praise and worship band, at least, and every other aspect of that place—church, yard, gym, amount of free time out of the cell, amount of exercise time, food quality, food quantity, educational and vocational programs, recreational activities, inmate commissary, staff attitude, every…single… aspect far outshined any prison I'd ever been in. Facts. Well, except for the SECOND discrepancy. Graham's healthcare was bad. Really bad. Their Chief Medical Officer was a man named Dr. Francis Kayira, and in this case the term "doctor" is used very loosely. The so-called nurses there, with a couple exceptions, were a squad of raging cunts. Politically incorrect and unacceptable as it is to use the aforementioned term in this enlightened era, it is, in this case, totes appropriate.

Healthcare in the Illinois Department of Corrections was classified as cruel and unusual punishment in the class action lawsuit Lippert v. Baldwin in 2018, and yet, in a department where substandard healthcare was the norm, Dr. Kayira and his nurses seemed to really go out of their way to mess guys up. But I didn't care about that. I was in perfect health. Ha! That's one thing about God. Just when you think you have life figured out He likes to throw you a curve ball.

So, to recap, I arrived at Graham in January of 2018. I wasn't the strongest guy on the yard, but I was 48 years young and able to bench 225 for a few reps. I was 6'1" and 210 pounds and could deadlift and/or squat 315 pounds. I could run for two hours or more if I paced myself, and I was still hanging with the 20-somethings on the handball and basketball courts. Respectable for my age.

All that was about to change.

CHAPTER TWO

Pre-Pandemic

The worst part of transferring to a new facility is where you have to discover that particular institution's rhythm and patterns. You have to get yourself in tune with a whole new vibe. It's not necessarily better or worse, it's just different. It ain't going to adapt to you, so you have to adapt to it. That's the worst part of transferring. To me it is, anyway.

At Graham I immediately joined the praise and worship team, or at least I requested to do so. Chaplain Daniel Shreve wasn't entirely a fan of mine at first. He was skeptical. Chaplain Shreve was a man of God above all, steadfast and faithful. He'd heard about me from several inmates the day I stepped off the bus. It seems that while my reputation as a Christian could use some work (and I am working on it), my reputation as a guitarist precedes me. I'm okay. But Chaplain Shreve, probably because of his past experience, was leery of musicians, particularly talented ones, who wanted to join the praise band. A lot of them were in it for the wrong reasons. Chap was all about the spirit.

The second thing I did to find my flow at Graham was join GrahamVets, another rehabilitation program for incarcerated veterans. It so happened that Chaplain Shreve was an Army vet (same as me) and was the GrahamVets Coordinator. I was moved into the Veteran Housing Unit in February of 2018. I was allowed into the praise band shortly after that.

One thing you have to understand about prison, and I'm talking about prison, not jail—jail is merely a minor interruption of one's life—is that prison can be a negative, mind warping environment that suffocates good and fosters evil. I've been in those places both psychologically and geographically. Behind the door in North II ain't no joke, and if you don't know what I'm referring to, then count yourself lucky. I've had my struggles. Prison can mess you up in all sorts of ways if you let it.

But at Graham I found a brotherhood, both in GrahamVets and in the praise band. I volunteered for the flag detail, posting the American flag in military formation every morning and retrieving it every evening. I didn't care that other prisoners would sometimes roast us as we marched by. I love this country and am proud of my military service. I became a staff writer for the GrahamVets quarterly newsletter "Behind the Lines," which circulated throughout the prison, other IDOC vet programs, and even outside VFWs. I devoted myself to the praise band, using my talent in service to God through music ministry. I found as close a sense of home and purpose that a person can find inside prison. You have to find that, whatever it is for you. Some find it in positive ways, others find it in negative ways, and some never find it at all. I found it in the praise band at Galesburg when I was there, and I found it in the band room at Danville. Having that "thing" in your life, whatever it is for you, is like having an anchor for your sanity. But at Graham it was something special. Something real. I'd still be there if not for what happened next. What happened, you ask?

One of those curve balls from God I was talking about.

Everything was going great. Then, in May of 2018, I started to get a hitch in my step on the right side and my right hand started tingling all the time, then went numb. Next came motor function problems in my legs and right hand. My guitar playing became affected. Then, one day in late May I was running laps on the yard and my right leg inexplicably went limp and I struck the track hard. It was a few moments before I could get up and limp away. Like most men, I tend to ignore physical ailments until they can no longer be ignored. When I hit the track, this was enough of an alarm that I finally went to sick call. Keep in mind that I absolutely HATE doctors, hospitals, and healthcare units. In the past 20 years I'd put in for sick call about nine or ten times, and most of those were just so I could meet a prisoner who was in another part of the prison. Sick call is how we trafficked and traded whatever we needed to traffic or trade. One of the ways, anyhow. Can't spill all the tricks.

The abbreviated version goes like this; they said, "Chittick, there's nothing wrong with you! Stop walking like that, you're not that good an actor!" Then it was, "Chittick, we're busy enough over here without having to deal with your bullshit! If you come to sick call for this again we're putting your ass in seg!" I continued seeking treatment, so they put me in disciplinary segregation. My body was dying, I was convinced I had cancer or something, and all I was getting from medical staff was ridicule and derision. I prayed fervently, but didn't get better, kept getting worse. I felt like I was beefing with God. You ever feel like you were beefing with God? It's not fun. I know the story of Job, of how God allowed Satan to put ol' Job through it just to prove to Satan that Job was a good and faithful servant. Nice way to look out for your devout follower, God. I know I'm supposed to trust God through all hardship, just like good ol' Job did, but if I'm being 100 percent honest, I was a little like, "What the H-E-double-hocky-sticks, God? This is how you do your boy? Are we into it right now? You wanna throw hooks, or what?"

Summer moved on, turned to fall. I was messed up, in constant pain, confused, and scared. They simply allowed me to suffer and refused any meaningful treatment. If not for my mother, Catherine Chittick, advocating on my behalf, I'd have probably never gotten an MRI. She raised enough hell to the powers-that-be that they were finally like, "Hey, give this frickin' guy an MRI to shut this lady up." That's how it works. They have to know you have someone on the outside who cares about what happens to you. I know. I was the Counselor's clerk for three years in Danville. The first thing they do when they go to resolve an inmate grievance is to pull his file.

"Does he have anybody on his visiting list?"

"No."
"Does he make any phone calls?"
"Nope."
"Does he send or get any mail?"
"None."
"Oh, then fuck him. We can do whatever we want."

PRISON WAR STORIES

When I worked in the Counselor's offices in Danville, I saw a lot. Here's one for you. Keep this on the down low. One day Counselor Jamie Tate was taking prisoner DNA samples. He'd give them a Q-Tip, tell them to swab their own cheek, then place the Q-Tip in the bag, seal it, and it was on to the next. Like clockwork.

So, a 6'4", 300-pound, black gentleman comes in then proceeds to unzip his pants and pull out his Johnson. Tate goes, "Whoa, whoa, what the hell are you doing? Put that thing away!" The large man apologized, saying he thought they needed to insert the Q-Tip into his penis to get the sample. Without missing a beat, fast as a whip, Tate replies, "Oh yeah, man, we do, we do. But I'm just the guy putting the information on the sample kit. When I'm done you're going to take this to that first door there on the left. Set it on Mr. Kiley's desk and drop your pants, he'll take the sample in privacy."

Counselor Kiley was a quiet, mild-mannered, and relatively small, white man. He always endured a bit of good-natured hazing from his fellow counselors. Kiley was a little quirky, but a good and decent person.

Anyways, this hulking black dude does as he's told, goes towards Kiley's office. Kiley was in there hard at work on his computer processing inmate visiting lists, entirely unprepared for what was about to happen. We watched. The man disappeared from our field of vision. Silence. Tense anticipation.

And then Kiley's normally quiet voice rang out loud and clear, tinged with panic, "Hey, guy! HEY, GUY!"

Graham had ignored me for months, claiming that I'd been faking, a diagnoses they based on absolutely nothing. The MRI revealed that I had a spinal compression in my neck due to two herniated discs. The compression was severe, and I was in danger of becoming quadriplegic and needed immediate surgery ASAP. I had the surgery on January 5, 2019 and spent January and February relearning how to walk. My neurosurgeon, Dr. Jose Espinosa, informed me that due to the severity and duration of the compression I'd suffered a substantial degree of irreversible neurologic damage, and he was right. I can't walk right and most likely never will, and I'm messed up in all sorts of other ways. I can't play any sort of sports anymore, and my musical virtuosity is a thing of the past. My right hand is smoked. I can still play, but it's a far cry from my old self. The worst part is knowing that I could have had a complete or near-complete recovery according to my neurologist, Dr. Yoon Choi, had prison medical staff made a prompt diagnosis.

This was a bad time in my life, and this is coming from a man who was sentenced to 28 years in prison. Whose sons grew up calling someone else dad. Whose wife had children with another man. The loss of my physical abilities hit me much harder than I let on at the time. The idea of killing myself was a constant. Even now that old thought will lurk on the outskirts of my mind, looking for a way in. Other, more sinister thoughts came, as well.

I went so far as to formulate a plan at one point. I wrote goodbye letters to the people in my life who mattered, gave them to a good friend to mail out for me, a fellow veteran. Told him he would know if it was time. I had gotten a razor blade. I took it to the yard and sat out by this light pole in the middle of the track field. Two vertical wrist slits and it would've been case closed. But I decided to take it to healthcare instead.

There was a particular nurse who'd set the tone from the very beginning of my ordeal. I won't reveal her name, but she'd been the one who'd decided that I had been faking my symptoms. Having seniority, her opinion spread like a contagion. She'd also subjected me to a significant amount of ridicule, both before and after my surgery. The revelation of my spinal compression seemed to anger her in that it had proven her wrong. It wasn't, "I apologize, Mr. Chittick. I was wrong." I overheard her say to another nurse, "Well, how did he even get an MRI, anyway? Who the hell okayed that?"

I don't know anything about her personal life, but I 100 percent guarantee that she has never been closer to death than that day I sat there with that blade in my mouth as she took my blood pressure. I was waiting for her to make one, just ONE, of her usual derisive comments. When she went to take the pressure cuff off

I was going to slice her jugular while her hands were occupied, then go into Dr. Kayira's office and take him out, then lay open my own jugular. The way I saw it, if I was going to take myself out, no sense in going alone. The officers behind the desk would never have been able to stop me in time.

My heart was pounding in my chest. Beads of nervous sweat formed on my forehead. My mouth went dry and I became worried about cutting the inside of my jaw or gums when I went to take the blade out. Then I thought to myself, "Who cares if you cut your mouth, stupid? You're about to kill yourself anyway! Say something crazy, bitch. Go on, say something. Say something! SAY SOMETHING!"

For whatever reason, she remained stone silent that day. Maybe she sensed something in my demeanor, but she saved my life. I could not bring myself to do it in cold blood, I needed her to instigate it, but she didn't or maybe I just punked out.

Sorry if what I just disclosed is shocking. I have a strict code about not hurting women, but I was going to make an exception in her case. When you go from being a fully functional and athletic person who enjoys life to someone who's in constant pain and can barely walk, you're going to feel a certain type of way, especially if you can point to someone and say, "YOU did this to me." Thoughts of revenge. Payback. It's human nature. The mind is a battlefield of right and wrong.

And yet, in order to be forgiven you have to be willing to forgive. It's one of the most basic tenets of my faith. The Lord's Prayer goes, "Forgive us our trespasses as we forgive those who trespass against us." In a nutshell, that prayer means, "God, if I don't forgive others, don't forgive me. Forgive me as I forgive." It's a prayer asking for God to show us a mirror; what you give is what you get. It's a dangerous prayer if you're not in the right place spiritually.

Double murder/suicide was not God's plan for my life. He put the right people in my circle to get me through that dark time. My fellow veterans. Art Garrison, who helped and encouraged me to work out, rehabbing myself. John Burton and Gary Swafford.

Carter and my other brothers in the praise and worship band. My brother Walter Edwards, even though he was in a different prison at the time, and his girl Shemekia Branch, who I emailed on a regular basis. And first and foremost, Chaplain Shreve.

A turning point was around April or May of 2019. The Christian band Fireproof came into Graham to perform. Their bass player had gotten stopped at the gate for some reason or another. He may have had a criminal conviction in his background. Whatever the case, Chaplain Shreve offered them my services. He did so without first consulting me, I might add. I really didn't even feel like being at the concert, not even as a spectator, I'd only come because it was expected of me as a member of the prison praise band. I was like, "Chap, my right hand doesn't work anymore, and I was only ever an average bassist on my best day. PLUS, I don't even know any of their songs." Fireproof's musical director was like, "We have sheet music, do you read?" Before I could answer (I was going to lie and say no) the prison choir Director, a good brother named Carter, chimed in, "Heck yeah, Nick can read music. He teaches music theory, he wrote a book about it!" I sat in with them. Peer pressure.

I had to sight read the songs off a music stand, which I hate to do. Playing guitar on stage while reading sheet music off a music stand is the musical equivalent of black socks and gym shorts; you can do it, but it isn't going to look good. But I made it through and did alright. I'm not sure why, but this event pulled me out of my swamp of self-pity.

Though I never completely disclosed the depth of my despair to Chaplain Shreve, I think he somehow sensed it. He prayed with me more than once and gave me a place in the church, allowed me to come over every day (almost) to rehab my right hand by practicing guitar. A lot of guards would also call me over to the chapel on Chaplain Shreve's days off and allow me to practice quietly in the studio room while various Islamic, Hebrew Israelite, and Odinist services were going on. It was technically unauthorized movement (inmate movement inside a prison is strictly monitored and regulated, as I'm sure you can imagine), but Graham was a medium security joint where the rules were a bit more relaxed, and

I was blessed with favor. I could more or less come and go as I pleased, which in prison is a luxury. The guards knew about what had happened to me and didn't agree with how it was handled. They knew about the healthcare staff. They knew about Dr. Kayira and his bungling quackery. It wasn't a secret.

By late summer of 2019 I had reached maximum physical rehabilitation. The degree of functionality I'd regained at that point, which was nowhere close to 100 percent (calling it 75 percent would be generous), is where I'm at now, pretty much, and where I'll likely remain for the rest of my life. I was frustrated and angry still, even if no longer homicidal.

I was blowing off some steam in an email to Shameeks (Shemekia Branch, my brother Walt's girl) when I texted something stupid along the lines of, "I know I'm a Christian, but when I see these nurses and that doctor I feel like doing some very un-Christian things." The message got screened and for the second time in as many years, and as in many prisons, I was called to Internal Affairs. I was told that they knew about my situation and that they understood my anger, but at the same time, they couldn't have me threatening the safety of their staff. They said since I hadn't outlined any specific threats against any specific individuals, they weren't going to issue me an IDR (Inmate Disciplinary Report), though I know if they'd wanted to they could've put me in seg for at least six months. The Lieutenant told me I was on the next vehicle smoking out of that prison and asked me where I wanted to go. The first thing that popped into my head was Jacksonville Correctional Center. They said, "Fine."

I felt good about the move. I'd signed a contract already with the prisoner rights firm Loevy & Loevy, they were going to represent me in civil litigation against Wexford Health Sources and Dr. Kayira, and they were doing so on contingency (they only get paid if they win), so I didn't need to be in Graham to handle the litigation myself.

The ironic part is that IA only became leery of me AFTER I'd come to terms with my situation. What I've learned is that if someone is making noise about what they're going to do, then nine out of ten times they aren't going to do a damn thing. If someone is quiet and withdrawn, not willing to talk, that's when you need to be leery. I was no longer a threat, but I see their side. They have to error on the side of caution.

I was Jacksonville bound. I didn't know it then, but it was where I would endure the pandemic. My brother Walt was down there, and it was a minimum-security prison.

All I can say is, it seemed like a good idea at the time.

CHAPTER THREE

Pandemic Pending

Iarrived at Jacksonville Correctional Center on August 29, 2019. Finally! After 20 years and some months I'd arrived at my first minimum security prison. When I limped off the transfer bus I saw my brother Walt standing nearby, watching the new arrivals coming in. I say "brother" because he and I are tight, not "brother" because he's black, although he does happen to be black. Huh. I guess "brother" works for him on two levels. Anyway, he was wearing the red shirt of an inmate worker. He hadn't been in Jacksonville long, but had apparently already gotten plugged into the machine. It didn't surprise me.

I first met Walt in 2007. He was the drummer in the Galesburg praise band, I the flugelhorn player. Kidding! I was, of course, the guitarist. Galesburg didn't have any drums, so Walt had to play the synthesized drum sounds on a Casio keyboard. We ran it through a PA, and if you closed your eyes you'd never be able to tell that there wasn't a drum kit in the room. We've played music together now, off and on, for 14 years in three different prisons.

PRISON WAR STORIES

Walt and I worked together as chapel clerks for a good Chaplain named Manny Rojas. He was a man of God. This was in Galesburg around 2009. We'd only known each other for a couple years at this point. As chapel clerks, one of our responsibilities was sorting through the request slips, separating them by category to make Chaplain Rojas' job easier; Christian, Jewish, Islamic, and other religious service requests, special religious diet requests, marriage requests, all like that.

One morning we were working away doing just that and I read a request that raised the alarm. I handed it to Walt, saying, "You might want to check this one out." It said, "Hey, Chaplain, your worker over there with the braids is dubbing tapes and selling them. Just thought you should know."

Now there wasn't but two of us working for Chaplain Rojas, and I for sure didn't have any braids, so that kinda narrowed down who the kite was referring to. Part of our music equipment in the band room was a dual cassette deck, and before you ask…yes, we still have tapes, Walkmans, and cassette-playing boomboxes in prison. Still to this day. Anyhow, Walt may or may not have had a side hustle dubbing tapes for guys. For a modest fee, of course. But I can neither confirm nor deny this.

Walt read the slip, then said, "Man, I KNOW this handwriting!" I didn't say anything, but in my mind I was thinking, "Oh, you recognize the handwriting? We see hundreds of request slips a week, but you recognize the handwriting? Who are you, the black Sherlock Holmes? Sherlock Homie? You an FBI handwriting analyst now?" The morning went on, Walt kept going through stacks of old request slips, comparing writing. I'm like, whatever. He'd take a break, then go through more. All morning he was at it.

Around one o'clock he slammed the snitch slip and another piece of paper down on the desk in front of me and said, "I know I ain't crazy! Check this out!"

I was thinking, "Just look at the papers and then you can tell him it's not a match. It's statistically impossible." Then I looked.

Same backwards slant on all the Ts. Same swirl at the end of all the Ss. Every single letter was an identical match. The paper he'd matched to the request slip was a choir application that all the choir and band members had to fill out. The guy who had tried to snitch on Walt was a singer in the choir, a guy who kicked it with us every day. He never had much of anything, and Walt looked out for him all the time.

I looked up from the papers, then said, "Walt...I'll never doubt you again."

The first thing I noticed about Jacksonville were the grounds; the place was very small. Anywhere you were standing within its gates you could see the entire camp. After the massive, castle-like cellhouses and sprawling complexes of other prisons, it seemed like I was moving onto a postage stamp. With five quaint, single-story housing units that held 200 men each, Jacksonville contained just 1,000 prisoners at full capacity. That's less than a single cellhouse in Menard.

What stuck out to me even more than the size, though, were the conditions of the grounds. They seemed neglected and uncared for. Weeds grew along the fence lines unchecked. There were tire tracks where staff golf carts had plowed through muddy ground and then slung that mud everywhere, all over the asphalt, after driving up onto the sidewalks. Patches of weeds and dead grass. Discarded bits of paper, wrappers, plastic, and other debris blew about, littering the unkempt grass. It threw me. Most of the prisons in the Illinois Department of Corrections, at least all the ones I'd been in, boasted grounds to rival golf courses in their immaculance. Jacksonville resembled a hobo encampment. I would soon find out that the appearance of the grounds was merely a surface indication of much deeper problems. I'd just arrived at a place where the administration didn't give a single solitary damn about anything that went on.

Officers ignored established administrative directives. There was one clique of guards there who wore these black hoodies with skull and crossbones logos on the back. Oooooo, scary. "JACKSONVILLE TACTICAL TEAM" was emblazoned in graffiti-style lettering above the skull logos, across the shoulders. It looked like a high school art project one of them had done, then they all pitched in together and had the local custom t-shirt shop produce the hoodies. For sure they weren't standard uniform, Springfield would never have authorized such a garment, but Jacksonville had their own way of doing things.

The leadership there, all the way up from the Sergeants, Lieutenants, Majors, and Shift Commanders to the Wardens, resisted guidelines from Springfield and ran things how they wanted. There was one particular Counselor in Clinical Services who had no official rank or position, no authority whatsoever. In prison hierarchy she was one notch above inmate, yet she set policy at the facility, dictated clinical service assignments and objectives, and barked orders at Correctional Officers and other security staff with the brazen swagger of a Deputy Director from the Governor's office. She was empowered to do these things because of who she was sleeping with. It was a soap opera. Much more on her antics to come, but I didn't know any of these things yet, not that first day. I only knew that I was beginning a new phase of my incarceration, and damn, was I ever right about that.

There were a lot of things that took getting used to.

The dorm situation sucked. I'd hated dorms way back in my Army days, barracks life wasn't for me even then, and I was 18 and wild. Living in a dormitory is not where I'd envisioned myself to be at this stage of my life. At least back when I'd been in Graham it'd been medium security, which meant that you'd had the freedom to be out of your cell all day long, but also the option to escape the chaos and have privacy by going into your cell if you felt like it. In Jacksonville there was no escape. Each housing unit had two decks. Each deck had five 20-man rooms with 10 sets of double bunks, five on each side of the room. There was only about four feet of space between bunks, and in your room you not only had to deal with your 20 roommates, but also you had a steady flow of 80 other guys from the other rooms coming in and going out at all hours. You might be trying to make a meal as some dude is drying off after getting out of the shower, standing right next to where you were preparing your food. You might be trying to sleep while a rowdy dice game is going on in the back of the room. No escape from the chaos.

After all the years I'd spent in prisons where staff and inmates alike were governed by rigidly applied rules and regulations, Jacksonville was a departure. It was a minimum security prison pretending to be maximum security, like a child playing dress up by wearing mommy and daddy's clothes. Movement was much more strictly monitored than it had been in higher security institutions I'd been in, and they enforced a no talking policy in the chow hall, an over-the-top practice I'd never seen before, not even in the harshest max joints like Joliet and Menard. Each cell house had an electronically operated fence and gate. I hadn't seen that since leaving Galesburg in 2011, and it was a textbook example of utter uselessness in a minimum security camp where the inhabitants were all going home soon. Let's face it, most of the men there—I say most, but not all—wouldn't squeeze an orange in a juice factory. Someone's relative must have owned a fencing company, that's the most likely explanation of the redundant fencing around the units.

The administration there didn't follow its own rules. For example, a man I know was issued an IDR (Inmate Disciplinary Report) for theft because he'd brought back a bag of ice from his job assignment in the kitchen. This was shortly after I'd arrived. It was a petty ticket in the first place, one that would never have been written in a real prison with real security issues to worry about. What was he stealing? Water? His supervisor had given him the ice, it was summer and hot outside.

At his disciplinary hearing, when he asked the committee to call his supervisor, the hearing officer told him, "Prisoners can't call witnesses on their behalf. The only witness allowed is one who'll testify as to your guilt."

When he corrected the hearing officer, stating, "No...we're allowed to call witnesses on our own behalf according to the rules of discipline. It's in the administrative directives.", the hearing officer paused for a moment, then responded.

"Well, that may be the rule...but that's not how we do it in Jacksonville."

Some guards were openly hostile to inmates. They could get away with this because they were dealing with prisoners who were close to their outdates and didn't want any trouble. It gave them a false sense of toughness. A 240-pound, all-muscle prisoner might go into the unit hub and ask a 160-pound weakling desk officer, "Are there any request slips?" and, depending on the guard, he was liable to get a response along the lines of, "I don't know and I don't give a fuck, get back on your wing."

I eventually adapted to Jacksonville's rhythms. I was placed in Housing Unit 1, Room 4. I was immediately greeted by several men I knew. That's the thing about those of us who've spent a lot of time in the IDOC (20+ years), you can put us in any prison in the state and we're going to know people there. It's an exclusive club that I wouldn't recommend joining.

I saw Jab, a man I'd known for 20 years and been in five different prisons with. Ollie, whom I'd met and worked with in Danville. Other acquaintances. In prison, relationships are formed with those in one's proximity because it's convenient. You may have many acquaintances, but few friends. Friends—true friends—are rare and valuable in prison.

In life in general, I suppose. Jab was a friend. Ollie was a friend. They had each signed witness declarations in my lawsuit against Wexford. This put a possible target of retaliation on their backs for something they were getting nothing out of. Acquaintances don't do that.

When I moved my stuff into Room 4 I was greeted by a man whom I'd gotten to know a little in Danville, but had been around for 20 years, since the early 2000s, back in Menard, Nelly. We both caught our cases in 1998 or thereabouts. Nelly was pretty much the alpha in Room 4, but then again, he's the alpha of pretty much wherever he happens to be standing. He's a big dude. He doesn't hang out and kick it, per se, so much as he sort of looms like impending danger. One of his many nicknames is Thanos, but he's actually a smooth brother once you get to know him. Unless you're a goofy, in which case I'd advise you to steer clear of him for your own safety.

As I was moving my stuff to my bunk the same thing that always happens in prison started to happen; people started sizing me up. It's only natural. I pretended not to notice what was going on.

I was like, "What's up, Nelly?" He was busy making some food, he had his mattress flipped up and was using the steel of his bunk as a prep area. It was a lot of food.

"Hey, Nick, what's up, man?" he replied.

I could feel an instantaneous shift in the vibe of the room. Something like, "If Nelly knows this old-ass white dude, he must be okay." The sizing up phase stopped immediately.

Nelly was like, "Here's how shit goes over here, homie. I know you been locked up awhile, but this is how we break it down in Room 4. We clean the room every Saturday, we all pick up our boxes, and everybody pitches in. If you walk on the wet floor you owe 50 pushups. This is a smooth spot, ain't nobody on no bullshit, you ain't gotta keep your box locked or none of that."

"That's all good," I replied, "but I'm probably not gonna be over here long. Walt's getting me moved over to Two House."

Nelly didn't say anything, but there was a look, there and gone in a flash.

"What?" I asked.

He looked up from his meal preparations but didn't speak right away.

Then he said, "I know Walt's juiced in and can most definitely make that happen, and I know he's your boy, but you might want to rethink that. I'm just keeping it real with you."

"Why? What's up?"

"Two House is where all them young, wild boys are at. They gonna be up all night, making noise, rapping and pounding on tables and stuff. Two House wild'n out.

"Yeah? Hmm…"

I didn't go to Housing Unit 2. I sent word to Walt to push the kibosh on the move.

Another thing that took getting used to in Jacksonville was the bathroom situation. Five sinks and five toilets for a hundred guys. Not ideal. Still, things came together for me fast there. Less than one week after stepping off the bus I had a job as the new chapel worker. Walt made that one happen. He had more juice than Tropicana. Chapel worker was a coveted slot because of its proximity to the gym. Unlimited daily workouts. A lot of guys who'd been there for awhile didn't like it, there was envy. Sucks to be them. No, I'm being nonchalant here as I'm writing this, but in real time I was telling Walt, "Are you sure? I don't want to step on anyone's toes." He wasn't trying to hear any of that. Walt was like, "They'll be alright. And if not, then that's okay too."

The extra workouts were cool—with my spinal damage I needed them--but the real reason I liked the chapel gig was so I could be around music. When I'm playing music, I'm free. The chapel worker I was replacing was a man named Mookie who'd been locked up for 30 years but was finally about to go home. He was a savage on the keyboards, and I'd actually been hearing about him from other prisoners in different prisons for a few years. "Nick, you ever meet Mookie? He's a BEAST on the keyboards." Mookie had heard about me too, though mostly from Walt, probably.

We were able to play music together for a few weeks before he went home, at least. He was probably disappointed in my playing. After my spinal injury it was nowhere near what it once had been. My right hand coordination was smoked, plus the electric guitar they had was an early '70s model Epiphone. It was like playing a two-by-four with strings, so that didn't help.

Working for Chaplain Kean was very different. On one of my first days I asked for some Windex. He sort of chuckled and asked, "What do you think you need that for?"

"Chap, the glass out here looks horrible," I replied. "I don't think anybody's done them in forever." The windows, I meant.

He laughed out loud this time and said, "Just relax there, guy. This is a prison chapel. I don't think anybody's worried about it, do you?"

That's when I knew Kean did things differently from Shreve. In Graham, Chaplain Shreve had had four workers. Every square inch of the chapel was spic and span, every pane of glass smudgeless. Glass so clean it was dangerous to birds. All the brass was polished to a high sheen, even the kickplates on the doors, every shelf dusted, carpet vacuumed. It was a house of God.

PRISON WAR STORIES

As you may have guessed by how I have spoken of him, I hold Chaplain Daniel Shreve in high regard. Here's why.

Shreve wasn't always a Chaplain. He started out as a Correctional Officer in...I'll just say another prison other than Graham. He worked with this one Correctional Officer who liked to wrestle around with a certain prisoner from time to time. This is a major, MAJOR no-no in the corrections business.

One day as they were locked in one of their forbidden bouts a Zone Lieutenant walked in, surprising them mid-match. The C/O saw the Lieutenant last second, so he pulled out his mace and sprayed this kid in the face, then body slammed him and slapped on the cuffs. His angle to get out of trouble was to play it off like a real staff assault. He planned to put a bogus case on this guy, adding new criminal charges and years onto his sentence just to avoid a reprimand.

Chap witnessed the whole thing and filed a report. The next day he was called to the Warden's office where the Warden and a few other higher-ups awaited.

"Do you seriously expect me to file this report with Springfield?" the Warden asked Chap.

"Either you do, or I will." Chap replied.

"So you're going to jeopardize your fellow officer's career to help a criminal get out of a staff assault charge? Are you sure about this?"

"Did you read my report, Warden? There was no staff assault. They were horseplaying. Right is right and wrong is wrong."

Chap stood strong. He got the kid out of trouble and the guard ended up getting in even more trouble for fabricating the charges than he would have if he'd just accepted the reprimand for horseplay with a prisoner. They fired him. After that Chap was hated and ostracized by his fellow Correctional Officers and other staff. They made his job as hard as possible and tried to force him out, but he transferred to Graham and became the Chaplain there.

His integrity is nonnegotiable. No way Chaplain Kean would have demonstrated the same backbone and principles in the same situation. Chap doesn't just talk the talk, he walks the walk.

THAT'S why I hold Chaplain Daniel Shreve in such high regard.

Not long after I'd started working for Chaplain Kean he asked me if I'd ever been in Danville. I said yes, I'd been there for eight years.

"Oh, then you must know Chaplain Easton."

I did know Chaplain Easton. I was not a fan. I told Kean the first part, not the second.

"Yeah," Kean continued, "when I first started here he was a big help, he taught me a lot about what I had to do and what I could get away with not doing as far as other non-Christian services. I was on the phone with him every day, he really showed me the ropes."

I didn't say anything, but I didn't know how Easton could possibly have shown anybody any ropes, the man was practically brand new himself. I remember when he and his wife hired into IDOC in Danville from Ohio just a few years prior, him as Chaplain. He wasn't great at his job, he walked this threshold of doing just enough to justify his paycheck and not a shred more. This is who Kean took his advice from. I know I'm not supposed to speak ill of the man of God, but here's some cold, hard truth about the kind of man Easton is.

Forgive me, Lord.

There was a keyboard player in Danville named Keith Owens, he played hymnal music at al the Christian services. He wasn't bad, his playing was a bit stiff and cold, he was no Stevie Wonder, but he was a competent journeyman of his craft.

At evening services, when Chaplain Easton wasn't there, he used to have to ask the guards to unlock the cabinet so he could get out the power adapter for the keyboard. They always told him no because…well, they didn't like him. After a few incidents like this he asked the Chaplain one day, "Hey, Chap, they never let me get the power cord at night. Can I just hold onto it so I have it when I need it?"

"Why certainly, Mr. Owens," replied Chaplain Easton. "No problem. No problem at all."

Of course, the guards stopped Owens for a shakedown as he was coming into the chapel for evening services. They found the power adapter.

"It's okay," Keith told them. "Chaplain Easton gave it to me."

The guards cuffed him up immediately and dragged him away to disciplinary segregation, him protesting all the while.

"But what'd I do? But what'd I do?"

The next morning three Internal Affairs Officers barged loudly into chapel just as Easton was sipping morning coffee at his desk.

"Chaplain Easton! Come out here now!:"

He emerged furtively out of his office, intimidated, as well he should have been. They were the same three Internal Affairs Officers I'd had to deal with during the "Who was fighting?" incident.

"Y-y-yes? C-c-can I help you?"

A large officer, a roid-rager named Gore, stepped closer, towering and scowling, a wall of muscle. Unofficially, he ran IA.

"Did you give inmate Owens restricted electrical equipment and give him permission to keep it in his possession?"

"Umm…"

"WELL, DID YOU!?"

"N-n-n-o sir, absolutely not! I would n-n-never!"

Everyone knew he was lying. The cord was locked in a secure cabinet, Owens couldn't have accessed it himself. And even if he could've, he wouldn't have. You have to know Keith Owens to get what I mean; here's a guy who didn't have the nerve to wink at a hooker. They gave Owens a major IDR and shipped him out of Danville on a disciplinary transfer. It's hard to feel bad for Owens because he was, in fact, a child molester. Now you know why the guards never wanted to unlock the cabinet for him. But still. Easton was bogus.

My new boss, Kean, had been trained by this guy.

Chapter Four

Pandemic Pending

Around October 2019 I received notice of an incoming lawyer phone call. Loevy & Loevy. I was psyched. Yes! What great news did they have for me regarding the progress they'd made on my case? I floated to Clinical Services that day on a wave of optimism. Surely vindication and justice were imminent. I went into the private conference room, sat, and waited for the phone to ring. My heart was all aflutter.

Ring ring. Ring ring.

I picked up the phone. "Go for Nick."

"Hello Mr. Chittick, this is [redacted] from Loevy & Loevy. Yes… well, unfortunately, I don't think we're going to be able to continue representing you going forward."

Continue? They'd barely even gotten started.

"Anyway, we do wish you the best of luck and…okay, byyye."

Click.

What the…? Who the…? Huh?

I returned to my cellhouse shocked. They all but said it would've been much better for my case had I been completely paralyzed. Lawyers. Loevy & Loevy are a well-known prisoner rights firm who have helped a lot of prisoners, but in the end it is a business for them. They usually do class actions; larger payouts. I could've raised up, went after them for breach of contract, but why bother? Had to pick my battles. Couldn't very well fight Wexford and Loevy & Loevy. David versus Goliath is one thing. David versus Goliath & Goliath is something else.

I went back and forth in my mind about just giving up. A lawsuit is a huge undertaking, and thanks to an evil law called the Prison Litigation Reform Act pro se lawsuits by prisoners were dismissed 90 percent of the time. As much a hassle as I knew it was going to be, I just couldn't let Wexford get away with it.

Dr. Kayira and his death squad of "nurses" have killed prisoners time and again, or at the very least allowed them to die through their deliberate indifference or sheer incompetence. Think what you will of we who are incarcerated, but we're human beings.

I had a friend, Cowboy, at Graham, an older guy I used to play handball with. He'd been having these seizure-like episodes for a few months or so, ever increasing in severity and frequency. The nurses at healthcare told him, "If you're going to keep faking these seizures you need to learn how they go because what you're doing isn't it." This went on for awhile. Then, after a bad episode one evening, he was taken to healthcare where he was ridiculed, laughed at, and ordered to go back to his cell. He was heard to say, "Man, these people are going to let me die in here." before going into his cell for the night.

He died that night in his sleep. Turns out he hadn't been having seizures after all. He'd been having micro-strokes. He suffered a massive one that night. For sure no one lost their job, and as far as I know no one was even reprimanded.

Kayira turned another guy into a vegetable, this was reported in Prison Legal News, the guy's family was awarded three million. Another man I know was forced to walk back from the healthcare unit with a broken hip. He was confined to his bunk for a week before receiving treatment. These are incidents that happened during the short time I was there. Another man had to have his finger amputated because the nurses didn't change his bandage for over a week and didn't know that an infection had set in. Dr. Kayira was even sued by Frank Lamas of the Illinois Board of Financial & Professional Regulation to have his medical license revoked, but he's still practicing medicine, messing guys up with total immunity. Wexford is being sued in every state they do business, yet time and again they are never held accountable.

I was without a lawyer now. I asked myself, is this fight worth the trouble? I went there in my mind, I actually asked myself, should I just give up?

Then I thought about Cowboy and the countless other souls upon whom Wexford Health Sources has inflicted suffering, injury, and death just so they can maximize profits for their shareholders. Give up?

Absolutely fucking not.

CHAPTER FIVE

Pandemic Still Pending

That large ship called time moved relentlessly onward over open seas, cutting a swath through the waters of the present, leaving in the past only the fading ripples of its wake as it bore down towards that distant future shore. I didn't plagiarize that. That's all me, baby. Pulitzer committee take note.

It was November of 2019, the holidays fast approaching. The fledgling coronavirus was making its initial forays through the population of Wuhan, China, weeks away from its debut on the world stage. My health issues persisted. Decreased gastric motility due to bowel paralysis. Involuntary muscle spasms. Spasticity. Twitching. Contractures. Pain. Cramping. Burning and freezing sensations in my hands and feet. It sucks. Having a damaged spinal cord sucks.

I awoke from yet another fitful night of intermittent sleep to discover I was getting a new celly. Well, "celly" is a term we use for cellmate, which would imply one is living in a cell. Jacksonville didn't have cells, they had dorms. I was in the bottom bunk and the new guy was moving into the top bunk, so "bunky" would be the correct term, technically. But we don't say bunky. We're not insane. We say celly like normal human beings.

He was a fast-talking young man locked up for second degree murder. The first words he ever spoke to me were, "My bad, pops, but I gotta move my stuff in here. I'll be out your way in one hot second, dad." Two shots fired about my age before we even knew each other's names. He was arrogant as hell. I liked him right off the bat.

His name was Joseph King, but everyone called him Hustle. He lived up to his nickname. Every prison has a guy or guys like him; he worked every angle in that place upside down and sideways. If you needed something, he was the guy who could get it. He was like Morgan Freeman's character Red in Stephen King's "The Shawshank Redemption." Great movie.

Sorry, a bit of a sidetrack here. When incarcerated readers read a book about prison or watch a TV show or movie, nine out of 10 times it's complete bullshit. It's what some writer with no real-world experience thinks prison or jail is like based on stories they heard, read, or watched. You know who surprisingly gets it right? Stephen King. Even in "The Green Mile" the supernatural stuff is believable because he really nails the mundane, day-to-day stuff. That's the trick. Sorry. Had to get that out.

Anyway, Hustle was like Red, only Hustle was white. We would endure the pandemic together and become very good friends, but in November of 2019 we didn't know any of that yet.

Aside from my nagging health issues, life in Jacksonville was going okay. As well as it could've been in a place like that. Playing music in the choir was alright, but not ideal. When Mookie went home we needed a keyboard player. Our bassist, LA (because he was from Los Angeles), switched over to keys. He was a competent player. The guards started calling him Elton Juan when they heard him play piano. There was a young guitarist named Red (coincidentally) who I'd sort of displaced when I'd arrived. He went back to playing guitar because you-know-who got moved over to take over the bass responsibilities. Me. You-know-who is me.

I wasn't thrilled about playing bass but being on a praise and worship team isn't about self-gratification, it's about being in service to God. Plus, I wasn't about to leave my boy Walt hanging, stuck without a bass player, and anyway, he wouldn't have let me even if I'd tried. I got to play guitar couple times a week in rock band, so I was good. Well, not good but... let's just say Walt better be lucky he's my boy. I probably wouldn't have done it for just anyone, in service to God or not.

One thing I try to do when I play bass is to be a bass player, not a guitar player playing bass. Any musician reading this knows exactly what I'm talking about. Guitarists usually make the WORST bass players. As a guitarist I can be a flashy thousand-note-per-second showoff, or at least I used to be before Dr. Kayira came into my life at a time when I needed authentic medical attention. But I was less confident on bass, even before my injury. I was a pretty basic in-the-groove player who could throw in a few runs and fills and hit a few slaps, so long as it wasn't too crazy. Now I could no longer use the fingers on my hand. I had to play with a pick, which isn't the correct way to play a bass. For the first few weeks Walt would look at me crazy when I'd miss a note by a fraction of a second. He could always hear it, he had to keep reminding himself I didn't have it like that anymore. Still, those looks made me try harder. You'll have to ask him whether I'm a good bassist or not. All I can say is I did my best. We praised the Lord, so it was time well spent.

Thanksgiving came and went. In early December I called my mom. You may suspect, due to the fact that I've already mentioned my mother four times in these early pages, that I am somewhat of a momma's boy. You would be correct in that assumption.

I'm not ashamed about it. I'd been looking forward to a visit from her for a couple months, she was supposed to come in early December. She'd visited me a couple times a year ever since I was first incarcerated, flying up from Florida where I'd grown up.

I called her one day, as I often did, and she informed me that she wasn't going to be able to make it after all. She was having what she called "some minor health issues." Nothing to worry about, she assured me. I would later find out that those "minor health issues" were that her COPD (which I didn't even know she had) was progressing to Pulmonary Fibrosis. A major respiratory illness with COVID lurking just out of sight on the horizon. She'd been on oxygen for some time, but I didn't know any of this. No one in my family told me.

A lot of times the families and loved ones of prisoners tend to shield us from bad news happening out in the world beyond our prison walls.

It's as though they feel we have enough to worry about in here, or they don't know want to tell us anything that might set us off. I know it comes from a good place, they don't want to burden us, but speaking for myself, I'd rather know. The visit I'd had in Graham from her the year before was to be the last time I saw her face-to-face. I'm glad we decided to take pictures. Looking back, I feel ashamed because I remember being slightly annoyed when she told me about not coming. Some son I am.

CHAPTER SIX

Pandemic Impending

I t was a new year; 2020 was upon us. It was going to be great! The rock band was rehearsing for an upcoming concert. I was preparing to put a clemency petition together for myself. I still had health issues, but I was on a keto diet and back down to a slim 210. Fifty-one with washboard abs. My physical therapy was paying off, I didn't miss a single yard or gym.

2020 was going to be the best year ever!

I'd been spending a lot of time in the law library researching how to proceed with my civil litigation against Wexford and Kayira. Even though I'd been doing legal work for nearly 20 years, I specialized in Post-Conviction Relief Petitions with a secondary emphasis on other criminal matters; Appeals (I actually have a case pending in the Illinois Supreme Court at the moment, dealing with the question of whether cops need to obtain a search warrant to go through cell phone records from the phone company; is the data under the provider's ownership or the user, and is it a new law or an old law applied to a new technology?) When my client asked if I'd ever appealed to the Illinois Supreme Court, I said, "Sure! Lots of times!" (This is my first State Supreme Court case.) Also I do Mandamus Petitions, Motions for Reconsideration of Sentence, all like that.

The closest thing I'd ever done to civil litigation were the few times I'd helped guys out with their divorces. In every instance, the wives had been trying to get over on the husbands because they were in prison. My best showing was when I got the judge to order the ex-wife to turn over the husband's truck, motorcycle, and thousands of dollars worth of tools that had been purchased with credit cards. Much easier to prove ownership when there's a paper trail. She was ordered to release the property to the man's brother, who would be accompanied by county Sheriffs. I won't ever reveal the name of a client when discussing their case—jailhouse lawyer/client confidentiality—but I wish I could have seen the look on the ex-wife's face in the courtroom. He was on telephone conference court for the proceedings. He told me that when the judge issued his ruling the wife's attorney was like, "But your Honor, Mr. [redacted] is in prison."

"Nevertheless, he has filed a timely response to the petition for dissolution of marriage. It is pro se, and it is just barely timely, but it appears to be in order. Is your client disputing ownership of these items he's requesting? Because, I'll be honest, his response is fairly generous to your client."

"No, your Honor, but…"

"My order stands."

"Your Honor, those items have been sold already."

"Well…that's a problem."

The judge ended up ordering that the marital home be sold, which my client had been willing to allow her to keep since she was raising his two children. The home was sold for about $80,000, half of which went to my client, plus she had to reimburse him for the truck, tools, and motorcycle out of her half to the tune of $25,000. He got $65,000, she got $15,000 and no place to live. A rare win for the incarceration club.

I have to be honest, that case was 90% luck. I won't bore you with a bunch of legal jargon, but when you file any sort of document or motion with any court, you're supposed to cite the statute under which you're addressing the court.

Like, "Now comes the respondent, Bozo, pro se, pursuant to ILCS 5/122-1(b), blah, blah, blah…" My problem was this guy didn't even talk to me until he had just nine days left to file a response in order to avoid the court entering a default judgment in favor of the wife. I had no idea what the Illinois Compiled Statutes were for dissolution of marriage, and neither did anyone else in my circle. Believe me, I asked. It takes at least a week to get to the law library to do research, and even with the mailbox rule (the day you mail it counts as the day the court gets it) nine days was cutting it too close.

Here's what I did; "Now comes the respondent, Bozo, pro se, pursuant to the appropriate statutes, blah, blah, blah…" It was a hail Mary, but it worked. The judge went for it. Another might not have. Judges are supposed to give pro se (people who are representing themselves in court without attorneys) participants more leeway, but they don't always do.

Limited as my area of focus and familiarity of the law was, being almost exclusively criminal and narrowly concentrated on post-conviction proceedings, I knew virtually nothing about civil litigation. I was aware that procedure was extremely important in Federal District Court and that one misstep could cause an otherwise meritorious claim to be dismissed. I needed to learn civil procedure, and I needed to learn it fast.

Luckily, my boy Big Swole, may he rest in peace, was in Jacksonville. He would fall victim to the pandemic, and I will tell his story in upcoming pages, but in January of 2020 he was alive and well. I'd worked with him in the kitchen in Galesburg back in 2008 or so, we were both cooks. He was shot by a guard in Statville Correctional Center back in the day. He'd been standing in his cell minding his own business when it'd happened. He sued the IDOC and won $50,000, and he did it while representing himself. He was the guy I needed to talk to about civil litigation.

We were in different cellhouses (I keep saying cellhouses. They weren't cellhouses because they didn't have cells. They were housing units because they had dorms. Cellhouses…force of habit), but our housing units went to yard together. I talked to him on the weight pile during his workouts at every yard. He was totally cool about it and I learned a lot from him.

Also, my boy, Nelly, who I was in Room 4 with. He was the facility Law Clerk in the law library and a certified paralegal.

I bothered the hell out of both of them for a few weeks in a row, but they didn't seem to mind. Neither of them was known for being Mr. Nice Guy either, but for some reason they put up with me.

You know, as I sit here typing this something occurs to me. Big Nelly is a legit dangerous man, reformed though he may be. Big Swole was a dangerous man. My brother Walt, a Christian and also reformed, but undeniably a dangerous man. Bam. Ju. Taker. Li'l D. The other Bam. Lots more over the years. I am friends with a considerable number of legitimately dangerous men. Huh.

Anyway, I worked hard and learned civil litigation. I tried, but couldn't get any new lawyers to take my case. Because of the Prison Litigation Reform Act, lawyers were reluctant to represent prisoners. But you know me. I soldiered on.

PRISON WAR STORIES

When I worked as a cook in Galesburg, Big Swole, myself, and a few other cooks would sometimes bring food we'd purchased from the inmate commissary and smuggle it to work. We did this a couple times a month.

We'd bring pepperoni slices, jalapeno slices, summer sausages, pasta sauce, and other stuff. Then we'd combine those ingredients with stock chow hall items like shredded mozzarella cheese and other staples to make the best pizzas you've ever had in your freakin' life.

Swole would make the crust from flour, milk, and salt. He'd roll the crust out, toss 'em in the oven, and bake them with melted garlic butter. Next, when they were starting to brown, he'd take them out again and coat them with pasta sauce.

But it wasn't regular pasta sauce out of the jar. It was doctored up something decent with oregano, garlic, and other spices out of the prison spice room. Big Swole's secret recipe.

After that came the chopped onions, green peppers, diced summer sausages, maybe shredded chicken, maybe shredded beef, whatever we had on hand. Top that off with a stupid amount of mozzarella, then cover the top layer with so many pepperoni slices you couldn't see the cheese.

There was this one guy who worked with us. He never had anything to put in on it because he was always broke, but we'd cut him in because that's just how we rolled.

On this one particular occasion he was being extra thirsty, kept going to the oven and staring in as the pizza cooked. We were like, "Get away from the oven, man, Sergeant Locke is working tonight. You're gonna get it popped off."

"Man, that bitch ain't got no jurisdiction in the kitchen. We in the kitchen. I wish he would come through here!"

"Just stay away from the oven, man!"

Of course, he didn't listen. Sergeant Locke came through while he was at the oven door.

"What are you doing?" Locke asked.

"Man, I'm making these pizzas!" he replied with his chest

puffed out and a scowl on his face.

Sergeant Locke calmly unclipped his radio mike, pressed the button, and said, "This is 2-7 (his call sign), I need the shift commander to the inmate dietary 10-56." 10-56 meant immediately.

An argument ensued between Locke and the young man and culminated with the young man wearing two things; a shocked expression on his face, and handcuffs behind his back. When the shift commander, a Major, arrived, Locke had the pizzas lined up on the counter with the kid standing by in cuffs.

Locke insisted that the pizzas be thrown away, and the Major told Locke to take the kid out of the cuffs. At least he hadn't named any names when Locke had wanted to know who all was involved in the illicit cookoff.

Sometimes assholes reach the upper ranks in various organizations, law enforcement included. More often than not, though, those who reach upper echelon positions are reasonable people with good social skills, i.e. they're not assholes. As it turned out, the Major was not an asshole.

"Man, those look and smell great." He told the young man. "If it'd been me, I'd have just made you give me one of 'em and let you keep the rest, but you know how Sergeant Locke is. Tell you what...eat as much as you can between here and the Dumpsters."

With the Major supervising the disposal, here's this guy who didn't have a single dime invested in the endeavor scarfing our pizzas down as he's walking past us to take them to the Dumpsters. And he was the reason they'd been popped off! He had to make several trips, chomping away as he walked by with us glaring at him. Six or seven of us were convicted murderers, and it was a couple hundred dollars worth of food on the prison market, easy. We hadn't been making them just to eat, a lot was going to be wrapped and sold in the cellhouses.

I'd been so looking forward to the event that I'd purposely not eaten all day. I can laugh about it now, but at the time I literally felt like crying.

The kid didn't get beat up, but we never looked out for him again after that.

CHAPTER SEVEN

Pandemic Creeping Just Around the Corner

The LTS Supervisor in Jacksonville was a man named Dakota Getz, he'd previously worked in Danville and was one of the four LTS Supervisors for whom I'd worked while there. In fact, he'd been my boss during the infamous "Who was fighting?" debacle. He was a good guy even if he was a bit lazy about his job. But I didn't hold that against him. Everybody who works for the IDOC is a bit lazy about their job. It's why they work for the IDOC.

Getz had played college football at Iowa State. He looks like an overfed Abercrombie & Fitch model. Ha! He'll hate that last part, it's an inside joke. If he ever reads this I'll be in for it. You want to know what the inside joke is, don't you? I can feel you wondering. Oh...okay. Be grateful I like you.

Not much to it, really. Getz is...I won't say metro, let's just say he's style conscious. One day when I worked for him back in Danville he told us, his workers, "I'm not coming in tomorrow, guys, just so you know."

"Why?" I asked. "Is Abercrombie & Fitch having a sale?"

I've used several variations of that jab against him over the years, and he always hates it. Usually he'll tell me, "Get the fuck out of my office!" It wouldn't be any fun if it didn't piss him off.

In all seriousness, though, he does bear a striking resemblance to Rob Gronkowski, the NFL player. Google him. Dakota Getz, I mean, not Gronkowski. Well...FIRST Google Getz, THEN Gronkowski. Next, observe photographs of each of them for comparison and analysis. There. Hope that clears up any confusion about that.

Anyway, I'd taught music theory under Getz's supervision at Danville. Brief digression here. I know I do that a lot, so I'll make it quick. I attained my certification as a Peer Educator in 2015 and facilitated classes like Anger Management, Inside Out Dads (a parenting class), TRAC I (a prerelease life skills court called *T*rained, *R*eady, *A*nd *C*apable (hence, T.R.A.C.) and other stuff. We did it under the direct supervision of trained Counselors.

I pressed and pressed for them to let me teach a music theory class. They said, "We would, Chittick, but we have no curriculum for that. There has to be a curriculum so it can be reviewed and approved." I spent a couple months writing a textbook called "Basic Music Theory," and I wrote a syllabus dividing the lessons into 12 two-hour weekly sessions, developed weekly worksheets, and three unit review exams. I took it all to them. Getz was like, "Yeah, you can teach music theory." It was something he knew I loved to do, so he let me start the class back up in Jacksonville.

So, going into March of 2020 I had stuff going on. I was learning civil litigation and preparing my initial pleading for filing in Federal District Court. I was teaching music theory. The rock band and choir were preparing for an upcoming performance open to the general population. Irons were in the fire.

Day-to-day life was a lot of things, but never boring. Jacksonville was like a Snickers bar; chock full o' nuts. Just in Room 4 where I was we had all the makings of a great sitcom. We had Gonzo, the neat freak, middle-aged, yet still dedicated to his gang, Latino cellied up with James, the slovenly, effeminate homosexual who constantly dropped food crumbs and other trash down onto Gonzo's bunk and area, sending him into regular fits of rage.

James fancied himself a jailhouse lawyer but was woefully inadequate in his abilities. He was always screwing up some guy's legal work. They would go to him, he'd mess it up, then they'd come to either me or Nelly to fix it. I hated cleaning up someone else's mess. It was three times harder than just doing the right way the first time. I'd usually tell them something like, "I'd like to help you out, but I'm really swamped right now."

Nelly was more direct. He'd tell them, "Man, get the fuck out of my face with that, go have that chomo help you, you shouldn't have gone to him in the first place." Every now and then James would make some grand declaration, "Man, I got them now! They're going to HAVE to let me out when I file THIS with the court!"

We'd be like, "Dude…you touch little boys. They're not going to let you out. Your ass is here to stay." Just to clarify, for any LGBTQ warriors out there, I'm not equating James's homosexuality with his pedophilia. James is gay, which is perfectly fine if that's your thing. He was into dudes in prison. Younger dudes, yes, but still within the bounds of societal acceptance. His pedophilia, for which he was incarcerated, was NOT okay. It was separate from his being gay. He was into wayyy younger dudes, well outside the bounds of societal acceptance. We're talking sub-Kevin Spacey territory here.

We had the developmentally challenged Tyree cellied up with the intellectually deficient PT. One of their arguments might go something like:

PT
(Gruff voice)
Man, how come you don't make your bunk? You need to start making this bunk.

Tyree
(Deep slow voice)
My momma said I don't need to make no bunk. If it bothers you so bad, why don't you make it?

PT
Oh, hell no, you gonna make it.

Tyree:
No, why don't you make it?

PT
No, you make it.

Tyree
No, you make it.

And so forth...

We had Uncle Drew, the aging convict who could have had his own spinoff show called "Uncle Drew Tells It Like It Is." We had JD, the white nationalist, Trump worshipping, ultra conservative, Republican meth manufacturer. We had Vok, the first-timer, skinny, scared, white boy. A group of straight up black gangsters (Flea, Snoody, Too Tall, Nelly, more) took him under their wing and made it their business to "toughen him up." They would pummel him with body punches and make him fight back. If he didn't fight back the beating was worse. Different guys would attack him at random times to "keep him on his toes." One time someone even got him in the shower.

Illinois is unique in the above anecdote. The way other states separate by race when in prison is not how Illinois is. Most of the prisoners in the IDOC are from Chicago, and in Chicago it's not about race, it's about where you're from. What neighborhood. You have whites in Latino gangs, Latinos in black gangs, blacks in Latino gangs, whites in black gangs...it was a free-for-all. People from other states like Arizona, Texas, or California who come to the IDOC are always initially shocked when they see how it is.

They look around and see all the races intermingled on the weight piles, the basketball courts, the dayrooms, and it blows their mind. They're like, "Am I in Bizzaro Land? What the hell is this? This ain't the joint. I don't know what this is, but this ain't the joint."

We had Rico Suave, a young Latino brother who looked like the cover model of a Mexican issue of Teen Idol magazine. He was pretty vain about his long, black hair. Hustle was a barber, one of his many hustles, so Rico Suave asked him for a haircut one day. "Just a trim," he said. Hustle's like, "Sure, I got you."

He then proceeded to shave Rico Suave's head damn near down to the scalp. It was a boot camp haircut. Rico Suave was depressed for days afterwards, walking around with no hair and a sad look on his face.

Every day was something new.

I guess I was the old white guy in the corner witnessing all the craziness unfold. Not a single one of us knew about the coronavirus that was already spreading rapidly on American soil or how drastically our lives were about to change for the worse.

CHAPTER EIGHT

Pandemic at the Gates

Towards the end of winter going into spring of 2020, there were a steadily increasing number of reports in the media about some new kind of virus. I didn't pay much attention at first. Apparently, it was something you might catch if you drank too much Corona beer. A flaw in the brewing process, maybe? Oh, those news people! You know how they like to hype stuff up and blow things out of proportion. Crybabies. I was sure it was nothing…right?

Around the time this was happening I got an odd email from my mother. In it she brought up the subject of my portion of assets in the event she should pass. This was out of the blue. We had never discussed this before, ever. Like…ever. It sent alarm bells ringing in my head like crazy. Of course, I called home almost immediately after receiving the email and demanded to know what was wrong. Why was she discussing assets and passing away?

"Oh, it's nothing," she replied. "I'm fine. It's just that your inheritance is something you should know about. I'm not getting any younger, you know."

"Mom, stop it. You're going to outlive us all," I said.

"Well…I sure hope so," she said. I laughed. She always had a great sense of humor.

"But you're sure you're fine?" I insisted.

"Yes, yes. Don't worry, I'm just fine."

Somehow, I knew in my heart, even then, that this wasn't true. But I wanted to believe she was okay, so that's what I did. In reality at that time she was on heavy dosages of oxygen and was having trouble walking from the parking lot to her office building at work. I didn't find any of this out until much later. I was being told the G-rated censorship version of things. As I stated earlier, this is something many prisoners go through with their families; sugarcoated news.

I'd worked for months preparing my civil litigation pleadings against Wexford and Dr. Kayira. In March of 2020 I sent my initial filings to the United States District Court, 7th Circuit, Central District of Illinois. Before sending it I nearly asked Nelly to give it a final look but thought better of it. I'd bothered him enough already. Everything was perfectly prepared, or so I thought. There is a saying in prison; always go with your first mind. I should have let Nelly take a look at it. We'll get back to why in a bit.

My case was assigned to the Honorable Sue E. Myerscough. I read a couple of her cases at the law library and had my mom Google her. She was a Democrat and seemed to be a prisoner-friendly judge. Yes! Finally, a little luck coming my way. It was looking like 2020 was coming up all aces.

The concert was scheduled for the end of March; Walt, myself, and the rest of the guys were looking forward to it. No one in Jacksonville, inmate or guard, could remember a time when an inmate band had been allowed to perform a concert for the general population. That was a shame because it happened in higher security prisons all the time. We were going to tear the roof off the place. I was playing guitar on "Sweet Child O' Mine," "Turn the Page," and "Wanted Dead or Alive," all songs I could play blindfolded in my sleep. Another rock guitarist, a kid named Hammer, was playing guitar on the rest of the rock set.

I would be playing bass on "Hotel California," which had an interesting bass line, at least. If I had to play bass, at least it was something challenging. All the gospel songs were challenging. Gospel is very bass oriented. The rock band was going to open, the praise team was going to close. Come for the jams, stay for the salvation.

Getz had ordered us some much-needed new music equipment with money from the Inmate Benefit Fund, it was on the way, and we were all hoping it got there before the concert date. A new drum kit for Walt, a Mapex, a new Fender Stratocaster (my preferred guitar) and Line 6 amplifier for me, and a new keyboard for LA.

Alright, before anyone loses their mind about tax dollars being spent on guitars and drums for convicted murderers, let me explain what the Inmate Benefit Fund is and how it's generated. Say a prisoner receives $100 from their family. The prison only gives that prisoner $75 of that money when he spends it at the inmate commissary and deposits it directly into the IBF. They could never get away with just taking it straightforward from a prisoner as he receives it; his people send him $100 and he gets a receipt for $75? It wouldn't work, guys wouldn't go for it. So, they're smart about it. They take it as you spend it so it goes unnoticed.

When a prisoner buys a $1 bag of white rice, the rice only costs 75 cents. The extra 25 cents goes into the IBF. They take it on the backend, but that's our money all the same. Jacksonville did roughly $2.8 million in sales for the 2020 fiscal year. The IBF was $700,000. It was supposed to be used for basketballs, footballs, soccer balls, weights, other sports equipment, art supplies for prison art programs, and yes…music equipment. But we were locked down for the entirety of 2020 because of the pandemic. They say they spent $500,000 of the $700,000 in the IBF, but I don't know how. You'd have to ask them what they spent it on. You can fact check the numbers I'm quoting here if you want. I got them from a FOI request. They're legit.

Anyway, as much as we were all hoping the music equipment would get there in time, it became a moot point. As it turned out, the gear did, in fact, get there in time. But it didn't matter.

On March 11, 2020, Jacksonville went on quarantine due to the COVID-19 pandemic. It was real now. It had migrated from our televisions, an abstract concept of a far away disease somewhere halfway across the world, to a concrete reality staring us in the face, affecting our daily lives. There was a strange dreamlike, is-this-really-happening quality to it all.

The prison was completely shut down; no visits, no school, no yard, no church, no anything. They restricted us to our rooms and bathroom only; no showers, no dayrooms. They brought breakfast, lunch, and dinner to us in our rooms. No movement whatsoever.

"Well…" we all thought, collectively. "Hopefully this won't last for too long." Yeah, right. We all know how that turned out.

I turned 51 on March 23, 2020, 12 days into quarantine. I was still foolishly optimistic and had high hopes for the year. With my lawsuit filed, I began work on my Clemency Petition. Clemency is when you submit for a commutation of sentence to the Prisoner Review Board. A time cut, in plain English. It was my second attempt. I looked like a pretty good candidate on paper. I'd served more than 21 years of my sentence. I was a military veteran. I'd received all sorts of certificates for the completion of various classes and programs. I was a certified Peer Educator. I hadn't received an IDR since 2008 and had been in A Grade since that time. Well, I did receive an IDR in 2012 for receiving a haircut in the dayroom, but it had been a minor sanitation infraction for which I received a verbal reprimand. I had a network of support available to me upon my release. As my friend Chavez told me, "Man, Nicky, if they don't give you clemency then nobody can get it."

To sum up the utter inconceivable depth of my denial; my lawsuit was going to be successful. My clemency was going to be granted. My health issues were going to heal and go away. My mom was going to be fine. The quarantine was going to be over soon.

Was I setting myself up for some soul-crushing disappointment or what?

CHAPTER NINE

Pandemic Tip-Off

Prison is not a pleasant experience. Not even in the best of circumstances. We were far from the best of circumstances. For the first week or so of the quarantine we were on total restriction; we couldn't leave our rooms except to use the communal bathroom, which consisted of five toilets, five sinks, and two urinals. We could not take showers or even use the phone. Mail ceased, too.

Take a bunch of restless convicts, remove all activity and programs, allow them no movement, and cram them into confined spaces 20 men to a room. It wasn't a recipe for anything good. Give them nothing to do, and in short order prisoners will come up with their own activities.

From day one of the quarantine all normal prison operations stopped. No more shakedowns or compliance checks. Officers no longer wanted to step onto the wings. They would count at the beginning of their shifts and bring food at meal times, and that was pretty much it. Without officer supervision, things went Wild West pretty quick.

After a week of no showers, no mail, and no phones, the guys in

Room 4 had had enough. We collectively came to the decision that we were going to refuse food until we got our showers, phones, and mail back. We tried to get the other rooms to stand with us, but that plan went south fast. The other rooms had no interest in taking a stand and instead turned on us.

"Don't go against these people! You're going to make them mad and they won't let use the phone!"

"They're already not letting us use the phones, stupid motherfucker!" said Hustle. "What the hell are you talking about?"

"Yeah, but if you make them mad they'll keep not letting us use them longer!"

This was their logic. Bitch logic. Don't get me wrong, there were plenty of riders in those other rooms. But they were outnumbered. It only works if everyone stands together.

I don't know what it was about Room 4, but we were solid on Convict Code. We knew that if you quietly accepted things and didn't make any waves, the administration would think, "Oh, look…they're being quiet. Hmm…they must be okay with it. Keep doing what we're doing."

We weren't okay with it. The situation turned volatile. Nelly lost his temper. It was the first time I'd ever seen him that heated.

"Fuck you mean we're gonna make *them* mad?" he said, pacing the hall between rooms. "They should be scared of making *us* mad! You bitch-ass niggas is in the way! We ain't taking them trays!"

"Who are you talking to?" came an anonymous voice from one of the rooms.

'I'M TALKING TO ANY ONE OF YOU BITCH-ASS NIGGAS WHO THINKS I'M TALKING TO THEM, THAT'S WHO THE FUCK I'M TALKING TO, NIGGA!" Nelly replied.

It was a precarious scenario that could easily have turned out much worse than it did. Men were on edge, wound up tight, and tensions were high. And this was barely one week into the quarantine. We could never have foreseen in those early days how bad things would get. It's almost amusing to recall our early reactions now because the situation got so far beyond worse. Men we'd known for years were going to die because of the way the Illinois Department of Corrections in general, and Jacksonville Correctional Center in particular, handled the pandemic.

Worse, no one cared, and the people responsible for those deaths are still at work earning their exorbitant pensions.

But we're not to that point in the story yet. On that day, the end of the first week on quarantine, Room 4 refused their trays. I'm not gonna lie, it wasn't easy to refuse that food. Our supplies were running low (at least mine were) and we didn't know when or if we'd be going back to commissary. A Lieutenant was summoned and came to our room. Clearly, he didn't want to be there.

"Nobody in here wants a tray? What is this, some kind of half-assed hunger strike?" demanded the Lieutenant in a loud, stern voice.

A tactic often employed by Correctional Officers (or in this case, a Lieutenant) when addressing an inmate issue is to respond with aggression...Grrr! The inmate or inmates will then respond in one of two ways; one, they will back down, intimidated, or two, they will respond with equal or greater aggression...GRRR!! In the second scenario the staff member will de-escalate, or at least they're supposed to. It's mandated in their staff directives.

"We don't care what you call it, Lou," said Hustle, speaking for the room. "Just know that we're not eating nothing until we get our phones, shower, and mail back!" he added in an even more loud, stern voice.

Our phones were turned back on and the showers were opened the next day. Plus, we got our backed-up mail that night too. Of course, the members of the "just be quiet" and "don't make them mad" club said, "They were going to give us back our phones and showers today anyway. Room 4 didn't do anything."

This is a perfect metaphor for life, I suppose. Everyone wants to reap the benefits, but no one wants to make the sacrifice.

The sheep are many.

The wolves are few.

CHAPTER TEN

Pandemic 1st Quarter

A recurring theme of the coming weeks and months would be Room 4's willingness to rebel against the petty injustices that kept cropping up throughout the quarantine. It became normal to hear someone shouting, "Aww no, y'all! Watch out, Room 4's into it with them people again!"

This brings me to a point I'd like to make. No prisoner ever *wants* to riot just for the sake of having a riot. Not that we were rioting. My point is, prisoners are just people. I know the general public likes to believe we are all evil sociopaths who torture and kill children and probably dine on their flesh. And I will give you that there are some truly disturbed individuals in the maximum security prisons who need not ever be released. But the truth is that most prisoners are just normal people who love their children the same as anyone else. We've made mistakes, but we're not monsters. If prisoners riot, they most likely felt forced to do so, were probably denied some fundamental right. That's the part the media never reports.

Look at my boy Walt. He's doing 30 years in prison because of something that happened when he was 15. He knew some boys, friends of his, who shot and killed someone. The witnesses and the shooters themselves all claimed that Walt had not been present at the time of the shooting. A dissenting judge in Walt's appeal, who was in favor of overturning Walt's conviction, wrote, "What more evidence does this court require to prove this young man's innocence other than the deceased victim coming back to life and saying, 'This is not the person who shot me.'?"

Walt was convicted under the legal doctrine of accountability. In a nutshell, accountability goes, "He's friends with the person who did the crime. He might have known it was going to happen or he probably found out after the fact. Maybe. Let's just say he did. He's as guilty as the shooters. Probably."

The accountability doctrine has been massively abused in Illinois, there are so, so many similar stories. Illinois prosecutors' evil abuse of the accountability doctrine to rack up dubious convictions in this state is another book in itself.

My point in relaying Walt's story is to illustrate what I said earlier. We're all just people. Prisoners don't riot for no reason.

Not that Jacksonville was ready to riot. Not yet, anyway. What did happen, and it happened quickly, was that without officer supervision those wimpy little minimum security dorms devolved into some semblance of a real prison. Batches of hooch (homemade wine) were made. Tattoo guns were constructed and operated 'round the clock. Dice games, poker, and fights. Take a man's activities and he'll come up with some of his own, like I said earlier. Room 4 and 1-A (our wing, consisting of rooms 1 through 5) made so many waves that Internal Affairs began to receive reports from the snitches who were terrified by their new environment. There was no one to save them. This is not what they had signed up for. They felt thrown to the wolves, which they pretty much were.

Officers came to our wing 50 deep. They ransacked our belongings, calling it a "shakedown." From our perspective it was a home invasion and burglary. They came into our homes uninvited and began stealing our personal property. What would you call it?

It wasn't all bad, though. They put all of us out on the yard while they searched our rooms. They kept us out there for quite awhile. They had not yet removed the weights, so we got a good workout in at least. I know the other housing units had to be looking out their windows saying, "Heyyy…how come they get to go to yard?"

While we're on the subject of yard, the administration's stance on denying us yard because they didn't want us getting too close to each other was utterly ridiculous. We were sleeping 20 men to a room with barely four feet between us. There was literally no place you could stand inside the housing units where you could be six feet from another person. A hundred of us sharing five sinks, five toilets, and two urinals. The yard was 500,000 square feet of open space. Maybe more. Then again, I'd been locked up long enough by then to know that trying to use logic and common sense to figure out the actions of the IDOC was an exercise in futility. The things they did rarely made sense.

After all their searching and tearing our homes apart, they didn't find *anything*. Jacksonville rookies. They came in between batches of hooch, for one thing. For another, they put us on the yard without thoroughly searching us. As the guards were looking for contraband in our rooms, the prisoners were working out on the yard with the contraband in their pockets. Internal Affairs chalked it up to their snitches giving them faulty information.

Small victories. Sometimes in life you have to take your wins where you can find them.

CHAPTER ELEVEN

Pandemic 1st Quarter

They called my name at 3 pm shift change one day. "Hey, Chittick, bring a pen and your ID to the bubble!" The "bubble" is the officer's desk at the entrance to the housing unit. This could only mean one thing. Legal mail!

Yes! My lawsuit with the evil corporation Wexford was now officially underway. Judge Myerscough had probably been so convinced by the iron-clad logic and unshakable legal foundations of my initial pleadings that she'd granted summary judgment in my favor, declaring me the winner. How could she not? I signed for it, went back to my room, and eagerly tore it open.

"Plaintiff's motion to proceed as a poor person in this case without prepaying the costs of litigation in this matter has been…DENIED."

Denied? What the? I read on.

"Plaintiff has received nearly $1,400 deposited into his prison trust fund account within a six-month period and has spent most of that at the inmate commissary. He therefore does not qualify as indigent under the law and should be able to pay for the cost of this litigation."

You've got to be kidding me. Let's forget that Christmas and my birthday fell within the six-month window they audited, undoubtedly exaggerating my average, causing it to seem higher than it was. Forget that this money came in the form of random gifts, over which I had no control, from family and friends.

Let's say, just for the sake of argument, that it was my own steady income, as Judge Myerscough apparently hypothesized. In what universe does an annual income of $2,400 fail to qualify someone as poor?

Secondly, why did she write, "He has spent most of that at the inmate commissary." Well, where the hell else was I supposed to spend it? The Hallmark store? What did she believe was sold at the inmate commissary?

I feel like I need to clear up a common misconception. The general public, at large, seems to take it for granted (erroneously) that prisons provide for all the basic needs of their prisoners. Allow me to assure you, they do NOT. We live in a capitalist society. Soap, toothpaste, toothbrushes, deodorant, dental floss, mouthwash, shampoo, conditioner, shaving cream, razors, laundry detergent, socks, t-shirts, boxers, gym shorts, boots, sweatpants, sweatshirts, gym shoes, thermal tops, thermal bottoms, hats, gloves, other cold weather gear, pajamas, Tylenol, vitamins, cold medicine, antacid tablets, writing paper, pens, typing paper, typewriter ribbons, folders, pencils, school supplies, phone minutes for speaking to your loved ones, all this and many more of the necessities prisoners require are sold at the inmate commissary. If a prisoner does not BUY these things, he or she does not HAVE these things. If someone you love is in prison, send them $20 today. You have no idea what a big difference that little bit can make.

I didn't understand. Did Judge Myerscough envision me squandering my meager financial resources to lie on a bed of Twinkies and cupcakes as I doused myself with Cherry Pepsi and Mountain Dew? I mean, a Motion to Proceed in Forma Pauperis is just a formality, and I didn't even make it past that. Most judges grant prisoners forma pauperis (poor person) status as a matter of course, unless that prisoner had bank accounts, real estate, or other tangible wealth. I didn't have any of that.

I showed the order to Nelly.

"Oh yeah, man. You should've shown it to me before you sent it in!

I'd've told you to wait a couple months before filing it if I'd seen your trust fund printout," he said.

I asked what the legal threshold for poverty was. He said when it came to prisoners, there wasn't one. It was whatever a particular judge said it was. Not only did the standard differ from district to district, it varied greatly from judge to judge in the same district.

This setback gave me pause and forced me to rethink my position. If I couldn't even get past a minor formality like a Motion to Proceed in Forma Pauperis, what would I be up against when I got into the actual litigation of my case? I needed more education. Formal education. The law library was closed indefinitely due to the quarantine. No more research or self-study. I couldn't keep bothering Nelly. What to do?

I'd been subscribing for years to a publication called Prison Legal News. Well, at least been reading it for years, if not always subscribing. In it there were always ads for Blackstone Career Institute. They had a Legal Assistant/Paralegal Studies program in which you could earn a certification as a paralegal. More importantly, to me, you could learn the law and the proper procedures to follow in civil litigation. I decided to enroll.

It was one of the best decisions of my life.

CHAPTER TWELVE

Pandemic 1st Quarter

I was lucky. I had someone who cared about me who was willing to pay my Blackstone tuition. I'll give you three guesses who it was. Mom. It was mom.

Around the time I asked her about enrolling was when I began to discover that her condition was more serious than I'd initially been led to believe. I was still getting a somewhat filtered version of the truth but learned that she was ill enough to have had to stop going to work. She'd be working from home for the foreseeable future. Not only did she lack the stamina to travel, it simply wasn't safe in the coronavirus era. With her COPD (I still didn't know that she had pulmonary fibrosis) COVID was a real concern.

After she told me about this she went on to say that I should probably prepare myself for lean times. With her uncertain work situation, she wasn't sure if she could keep depositing money into my prison account. Like *that's* what I cared about.

"Mom, forget about money on my books and fuck Blackstone. You just get yourself healthy and be safe out there. I'll be fine," I said.

"No, no, I'm going to pay your tuition," she replied. "I want you to take that class. You should've taken something like that a long time ago. It'll be good for you. And don't you worry about me, either. I'm going to be fine too."

I'll never forget the feeling I had after hanging up on that call. I was adrift in uncharted territory, all these massive forces circling my life at once. The pandemic and how it had shifted the world's reality. My changed physical status and ongoing health issues stemming from my spinal damage. The lockdown and the pressure tensions it was generating. A complicated medical lawsuit against a powerful for-profit healthcare corporation with an army of seasoned litigators at their disposal, a Titan nemesis who were a well-oiled machine of denying their victims justice. The new discovery of my mother's own health issues, which railed against all I knew. She had maintained healthy body weight her entire life, had stopped smoking decades ago, and had ridden bicycles into her 60s. She was supposed to be healthy. Officers were wearing surgical masks. I was unmoored from the truth of real life, it was as though I had accidentally stepped through an invisible portal to an alternate dimension. It looked the same, but this was not my universe. We were all going through this mind warp together, and like many others, I put up a front and pretended everything was everything. That's what you do in prison.

About the time George Floyd was murdered by Minneapolis police officer Derek Chauvin, prisoners in the IDOC were mandated to wear masks. We were given one per week. Saturday became known as "Mask Day."

They began allowing us to walk to the chow hall again for our meals. It was a welcome decision, a small, incremental step back towards normalcy, though we were now required to sit one to a table where it had been four.

I was going insane sitting in the housing unit every day with nowhere to go and nothing to do. I decided to put in for a job in dietary. Hustle put in a good word and I was in.

I only worked there for a few weeks. It was dangerous for me to be a cook, carrying scalding hot liquids, working near open friers, and stirring those boiling 80-gallon kettles on my unsteady legs. But that's not why I quit.

I quit my job in dietary because of the person in charge of dietary. Ms. White was her name, and she was...see, I know I'm not supposed to use this word, but she was a...hmm. I'm sorry. I'm not a sexist. Sometimes it's the only word that fits. Ms. White was a total cunt. Point blank.

By all accounts food quality and portion size had suffered an exponential decline under her watch. I'm sure the food budget for Jacksonville also dropped a lot during her tenure, so her bosses probably felt she was doing a great job. If I had her address I would post it within these pages and ask each reader to send her a short note asking her to stop being such a bitch. Oh wait, I actually do have her address. Let's do it. It's...

JOLENE WHITE

123 SPENCER AV...

No, just kidding. But wouldn't that be awesome? I don't even know if Jolene is really her first name. She just seems like a Jolene to me for some reason. I'm trying not to come off as bitter and angry, but it's hard because I am, in fact, a little bit bitter and angry. I can admit it. A person has to know their self. Honest self-assessment is difficult, but necessary for positive growth.

Back to dietary supervisor White. You remember her. The cunt? Yes. There was a large donation of ice cream made to the prison about the time I started in the kitchen. It was just ever so slightly past its expiration date. By a few years. No, not that much, but it wasn't fresh. Even so, it was an exceedingly rare treat for us. Like freakin' manna.

Ms. White doled it out to the staff like it was going out of style. She gave unlimited portions to the inmates working in dietary too, but it didn't make a dent. There were a couple pallets of five-gallon containers of the stuff. She could have served it to the entire prison three days in a row. For whatever reason (I think we all know why...it starts with the letter c) she refused to serve it to the general population. She ordered it to be thrown away. That's just how she is. Fortunately, not all staff are vindictive cu...people. Weren't we suffering enough? We were on lockdown, not getting visits, church, yard, school, or any other movement or activity whatsoever.

The only relief prisoners were getting from the jam-packed cellhouses was coming to the chow hall. One dietary supervisor (who shall remain nameless because I don't want them to get into trouble) decided to defy Ms. White's orders. Could have been any one of them. Maybe a guy. Maybe a gal. Maybe a 5'3" gal with blonde hair whose last name started with R. Anyone, really.

She, I mean the dietary supervisor in question, waited until the weekend when Ms. White was off and then served the cool treat in crazy generous portions, piling it onto the trays in defiance of Ms. White's explicit instructions.

Prison can be a place of harsh cruelty, shocking violence, and petty torments. But it can also be a place of surprising generosity, acts of kindness, and small mercies. We're all just people, staff or inmate. Some are good, some are bad. Just people.

A little expired ice cream didn't seem like too much to ask in the face of a worldwide pandemic.

Chapter Thirteen

Pandemic 1ˢᵗ Quarter

Spring was coming to an end and summer was nearly upon us. Weather was getting hotter. Maybe that will kill off the virus, we all thought. Yeah, okay. We all know how *that* turned out.

About this time a prisoners' rights organization known as the John Howard Association came to check on our wellbeing. I still don't know who John Howard was or why he cared about our rights, but I'd been familiar with their work since the late '90s. They got stuff done.

One of the first things they asked was whether or not we were getting enough yard. Yard? We hadn't seen the yard in over two months. That changed immediately. Soon after JHA got involved we were allowed to go to the yard one room at a time in groups of 20.

The weight pile was closed, but there were heavy wooden picnic tables under the pavilion. Prisoners are nothing if not resourceful. We quickly devised several ways to work out with them. I got in a few sets of picnic table bench presses with Uncle Drew. Nelly and his crew were doing them with people lying down on top of the tables, but Uncle Drew and

I did ours without the extra body weight. I felt pretty good for a half-cripple who hadn't worked out in over nine weeks. It was a warm day. Maybe a little more than warm. I decided to cap off my workout with a few laps around the ol' track. I wore a sweatshirt and a skull cap so I could get in a good sweat. What could go wrong?

I set a nice slow pace. Ah, who am I kidding? Nice and slow was the only pace I was capable of setting. I wouldn't call what I did anymore *running*, not in the strictest sense of the word. It's more of an awkward, right-foot-dragging lurch. A good speed walker could have passed me. But I did a couple few laps, got a good sweat in. I went back to the housing unit out of breath but otherwise fine. I was standing in the line, waiting on the showers. That's when things went south.

Stars began to swirl in my field of vision. No big deal. I went to the benches to sit down and catch my breath. Hoo boy. I sure was sweating a lot. Buckets. I couldn't catch my breath. And why was it so hot in there? The A/C was blasting, but I was burning up.

The room suddenly went sideways on me. I could see Rico Suave doing calisthenics in the corner. I called out to him. He ignored me. I called out again, louder. Why was he ignoring me? I waved my arm and got his attention. He came walking over and I realized I was lying on the bench. When had I gone from sitting to lying down?

"Damn, Nick, you don't look so hot," said Rico. "Are you alright?"

"Why certainly, my good fellow. I am perfectly fine, in splendid health, thank you for asking. Say, if it shan't be too much of a bother, do you think that you may perchance provide me with some cool, refreshing water?"

"What?"

"I said, do you think you might obtain some water for me, good chap?"

"I can't understand you, you're moaning."

"Water," I said, with as much enunciation and diction as I could muster.

"Are you saying water?"

I nodded my head yes.

"Where's your cup?"

"You shall find my drinking cup sitting precisely in the right recess of my shelving unit, next to the…"

"Never mind, I'll find it myself," said Rico.

Rico returned a moment later (or it could have been an hour for all I know) with a cup full of cool, refreshing water. Lying on my back, I opened my mouth to take a drink and proceeded to poor the entire cup over my face and head. Fuck it, close enough.

"Tricky Nicky, you're messed up, man. I'm going to go get those people," he said.

Sounded okay to me. I gave him the thumbs-up sign.

"Are you saying thumbs up, you're okay? Or are you saying thumbs up, go get them people?"

Damn it, Rico. Really making me work here. With gargantuan effort, I raised my hand and pointed to the exit, then gave the thumbs-up sign again.

"Thumbs up, go get them people?"

Killing me, Rico. You're killing me. I nodded my head yes, and Rico was off.

Officer Edwards came in. He was saying something, but I suddenly remembered my watch, shoes, and clothes hanging unattended by the showers.

"Hustle!" I called out. He would get my belongings and make sure they were placed in my property.

"What's up, dad?" I heard Hustle say. I could hear his voice, but I couldn't see him. Dang it. What was I going to tell him again?

Here I am relying on the account of others because I apparently lost consciousness. I have hazy, distant memories of C/O Edwards speaking to me, then a nurse, then blackness.

By all accounts I was as white as a sheet and my lips were blue. The general consensus was that I was either dead or in the process of dying. They hooked me up to the paddles and were about to shock me when Edwards politely pointed out that I was lying in a giant puddle of water, soaked head to toe, and drenched in sweat. I believe the direct quote was, "He's lying in a pool of water, you fucking idiots, are you trying to kill the fucking guy?"

I awoke in the back of an ambulance. There was a paramedic talking, but I couldn't understand what he was saying. He sounded like Charlie Brown's teacher. I distinctly remember looking around and thinking, "So this is what the inside of an ambulance looks like. Cool." It's one of those things you always wonder about.

I hadn't had a heart attack. The ER doc said I'd suffered a sudden drop in blood pressure to a dangerously low level due to dehydration. He called it a cardiac episode. I bet I was dehydrated; I'd sweated out every last drop of perspiration in my body. I didn't know we had that much sweat in us. The ER ran a few tests, gave me some intravenous fluids, and sent me back.

Jacksonville kept me in the infirmary overnight, then kicked me out to population the next day. I will say this about Jacksonville's nursing staff; they were nothing like the perpetually menstruating psychopaths at Graham. Jacksonville's nurses were polite, courteous, and professional, all traits frowned upon by Wexford.

By the time I got back to my housing unit the story was that I'd died and been resuscitated three times. Inmate Twitter. It's right sometimes, it's wrong sometimes. 50/50. I went to my job assignment in dietary that day. I saw C/O Edwards.

"Chittick, what the hell are you doing at work? Didn't you hear? You died yesterday," he said.

"I guess I should thank you, Edwards. They tell me you saved my life when you stopped them from shocking me while I was soaked in all that water."

"Yeah, our healthcare staff. Bunch of fucking idiots," he said, then went on about his business.

Walt sent word from Housing Unit 2. He was pissed. Nelly yelled at me too. I got scolded.

"Man, it's hot as hell outside and you out there running with a skully and a sweatshirt," said Nelly. "You ain't 20 no more, dude! You're trippin'."

"He ain't even 40 no more," added Hustle. They were ganging up on me.

"Right!" Nelly continued. "And it's our first day back? We ain't been on the yard in weeks! Don't do that shit no more."

So, I got checked. But still, it's nice to feel cared about. If they don't care, they don't say anything.

CHAPTER FOURTEEN

Pandemic 1st Quarter

The pandemic kept on. A large segment of the general public still refused to take the coronavirus seriously. Easter had come and gone. Summer was upon us.

The first two books of my Blackstone paralegal course arrived. "Introduction to the Law" and "Contracts I." A fellow jailhouse litigator who was familiar with the course warned me that the books were mind numbingly boring, but I thought they were great. The development of the common law in medieval England and its evolution in colonial America. Landmark decisions then that impact the interpretation of the law even today. It was sweet.

Don't tell anyone, but I'm a nerd in real life. I like learning stuff, I love "Star Trek" in its many iterations, I watch "Rick and Morty," and I dream of one day attending Comic-Con. My brother Josh and my mom attended Comic-Con a few years back. They attended a "Walking Dead" panel dressed as Carol and Negan, which I thought was a little off because those are two characters who would never be hanging out in the

"Walking Dead" universe. At least not in the time period they attended. They got to meet the real Carol, Melissa McBride, and take a picture. Totes awesome. I was jelly like a mofo fo sho.

Shortly after I began to tackle the subject matter in "Contracts I," I learned a little more about the grave nature of my mother's condition. She needed a transplant. Nothing major, just your minor, every day, run-of-the-mill LUNG TRANSPLANT. It came as a shock, as I'm sure you can imagine.

"A lung transplant, mom? For COPD?"

"Well, it's pulmonary fibrosis."

"What? Doesn't that take a long time to develop?"

"Well...it's pretty advanced," she disclosed.

Have you ever learned information that completely shattered your perception? A prisoner who believes his wife is faithfully waiting for him finds out she has been living with another man for two years and has bore his child. A man is about to be released after 15 years in prison. He finds out the night before his release that his prized possession, a Harley-Davidson motorcycle that his family had sworn to keep polished and ready for his release, had been sold by his brother while he was still in the county jail, about two months into his 15 years. A man who believes he is about to parole to his family home finds out when he submits his parole plan that the house had burned down nearly a year ago.

All three of those things happened, I know the men they happened to. I don't understand why our families do this to us. I suppose it comes from a place of love, but it's so much worse when we find out the truth like that. I don't know if I can accurately describe how it feels. When I learned about my mom it was as though the ground transformed beneath my feet. What'd I'd thought was solid turned out to be quicksand, and I was sinking.

On the plus side, my prayer life, which had fallen off as of late, increased dramatically. Seems like we pray more when we have something to pray for other than ourselves.

My lawsuit against Wexford was stalling. Judge Myerscough had ordered me to pay the filing fee, but I couldn't afford it. It was ironic. I could have foregone the Blackstone tuition and paid the filing fee, but I wouldn't know what I was doing. I had chosen to forego the filing fee and study the law to better represent myself in court, but because I couldn't pay the filing fee there might not be any court to represent myself in. It was a classic catch 22.

At any rate, my mind wasn't in it. I had a hard time concentrating on anything, my Blackstone books sat unread for a couple weeks. They even ended up sending me a letter to encourage me to continue on with the course, but I was very worried about my mom. I was powerless to do anything to help her. I was going through it, as the kids say.

One thing about being in prison--everybody has problems. The last thing anyone wants to do is listen to someone else whine about theirs. I had friends I could talk to, people like Ollie, Nelly, or Hustle, or to a lesser degree, others, but they had their own stuff going on. I'd already whined far too much about my ongoing health issues.

The one person who I *would* have talked to about this stuff, Walt, was in another housing unit and going through his own troubles over there. I knew he would have understood because he'd just lost his grandmother a few months back, the woman who'd basically raised him after his mother passed away when he was a boy of 12.

The troubles Walt was going through had to do with being in prison during the pandemic. Shortly after quarantine they'd begun issuing alcohol-based hand sanitizer to the chow hall so they could spray prisoner's hands as they came through for meals. Almost the moment it began being used, inmates started stealing it.

Some sister-banging rednecks in Housing Unit 2 had devised a half-assed filtration system for the hand sanitizer so they could drink the stuff. Walt had a front row seat for this; every day and night was drunken, brawling lunacy. Officers were no longer enforcing rules, so as long as you weren't burning down the place, killing each other, or blatantly doing something wrong right in front of them, you had a free pass to do whatever.

I've been known to partake of a good batch of hooch now and again, but even I—a devout lover of distilled spirits if ever one walked—will not drink hand sanitizer. How stupid do you have to be to do that?

Listen to me, the guy who used to smoke piles of crack, then when the crack was gone would pick up pieces of lint and God only knows what else, put it in the pipe, and smoke it. What right do I have to be judgy about what those stupid idiots were putting into their bodies? Still...hand sanitizer? No thanks.

This is what Walt was having to deal with on a daily basis. The situation also affected our friend Big Swole.

Big Swole had a black Panasonic radio. A jam box, basically. They had stopped selling them in the IDOC quite a long time ago. If you had one, that meant you'd been locked up for more than a minute. I caught my case in '98 and went to Joliet in '01, and I didn't have one. I just missed them, they stopped selling them right before I came in.

Anyway, Swole was kicking back with some homies listening to some old school hip hop. That's when one of the drunken hillbilly rejects decided it was time for him to make his mark on the world. Picture this; Big Swole was...well, his name says it all. Swole was a big, swollen up guy. He could have played John Coffey in "The Green Mile." The redneck (I don't know his name) was a scrawny guy with a long, scraggly, moonshiner beard. He looked like Pa Kettle's more redneck kinfolk from deeper up in the hills where they spoke banjo instead of English.

Hammered on hand sanitizer, ol' Billy picked up Swole's radio and said, "Fuck you and yer goddamn jungle bunny, nigger music!" or something to that effect, then struck Swole over the head with his own Panasonic.

I suppose Billy had envisioned the radio shattering into a thousand pieces as Swole went to the floor, knocked out. In reality, the radio did not even break, and the blow had all the effect of someone politely tapping Swole on the shoulder.

Swole got calmly to his feet. Billy's eyes widened as Swole's ham-sized fist came towards his beard-covered chin in the form of a right cross.

The beard wasn't much protection; Billy went down like a sack of potatoes, out cold. Billy's drunken companions tried to come into the room to retrieve their unconscious buddy. Swole's crowd wasn't having it. It was a classic prison white-versus-black racial standoff type situation. The whites in this particular instance decided that Billy wasn't worth the effort. They could have told the guard in order to save their friend further damage, but they didn't.

After a few minutes, Billy came to, dazed and confused. Swole helped the man to his feet.

"There you go, man. Easy does it," said Swole, placing a friendly hand on the man's shoulder to steady his wobbly legs. "You alright now?" Swole asked. A drunken nod yes was all Billy could manage in response. "Good, good. Here you go, take this with you," said Swole.

BAM! An uppercut from Swole connected under Billy's chin, rocking his head violently back and lifting his feet off the ground. The man's head struck the floor before his ass did. The man's friends (or supposed friends) were aware of his plight but did not come to his aid. As I stated earlier, true friends in prison, or in life, are a rare and valuable thing. Billy makes an excellent example of why this is so.

The same series of events played out again and again over a long period of time. The only variable was the type of punch Swole would throw; jabs, left hooks, straight-arm jabs, backhands. Swole mixed it up. I think one was even an open-handed slap.

This was a fight that could not go unnoticed because by the time Swole was done Billy was in dire need of professional medical attention. Just as I had a few weeks earlier, Billy was going to find out what the inside of an ambulance looked like. Or maybe not. I'm not sure when he regained consciousness.

Rather than allow his homies to face heat from the guards, Swole presented himself to the C/Os and took responsibility for the epic beatdown. We call this *taking your weight*. It's the kind of man Swole was. Integrity. He was taken to disciplinary segregation.

More than a month later I saw Billy coming through the chow hall. He was still so marked up that he looked as if he'd only taken the ass-kicking a day or two prior. He'd undergone one of those once-in-a-lifetime, personality-altering beatings.

I know one thing. Billy should be very grateful that Swole wasn't on some other stuff. Some freaky stuff, I mean. He would've gotten himself impregnated.

A word of advice. If you're ever in prison and you find yourself in a dorm setting, be aware. Should you happen to step into someone else's room, a room you're unfamiliar with, and you hear someone shout...

"Boy, get out of there, they on that up in there!"

Don't stall to ask questions. Leave that room immediately. I'm giving sound counsel here. Heed it.

Chapter Fifteen

Pandemic 1st Quarter

One day Counselor Lewis called me out to her office. I could not go inside because of the new COVID rules, which changed and evolved every day. I had to stand behind a yellow line of tape on the floor near the doorway wearing a mask.

"Hey, Ms. Lewis," I said. "What's up?"

"Hey, Chittick. Listen, we're preparing to start up a new program here. It's a peer mentoring program, we're going to train inmates to facilitate groups like anger management and conflict resolution for program participants."

"Sounds like the Building Block program in Danville," I replied.

"Yes!" she said. "It's based on that, actually. Are you familiar with the Danville program?"

"Yeah, I was down there when they came up with it. I know the three guys who basically created it, prisoners, Jersey, Six, and Mr. Hudson."

"Funny you should say that because 20 inmates here have been chosen based on staff recommendations to be trained as mentors. Your name came up. Does that sound like something you might be interested in?"

"Oh, God no," I replied. "That sounds horrible. I can't think of anything I'd be less interested in."

"You know inmate Edwards from Housing Unit 2, right?" she asked.

"Who, Walt? Yeah, what about him?"

"I've already spoken to him, and he's agreed to be a mentor. He wanted me to relay the message that you're doing it too."

"Walt said that?"

"Yes. He did."

Sigh. Tsst.

"Yeah. Sure. Okay, I'm in."

I have very few people in my life who I know for a 100 percent certainty have my back no matter what. My brothers weren't among that number. My own sons weren't among that number. Walt *was* one of those within that small circle.

What kind of man would I be if I did not have his back in this small thing?

The mentors began training in the academic building in early June of 2020. Of the original 20, three dropped out before training even began, bringing our number to 17. Seventeen out of roughly 1,000 prisoners. We were the only people in the entire prison getting any kind of academic activity. School had been shut down indefinitely. Quarantine was still very much in effect.

We were only able to do this because the peer mentor program had the full support of Warden Roberson. It was his pet project.

Another one of my brief digressions here. I know, I know. I do this a lot. Bear with me.

I did not like Warden Roberson. He had banned the final season of "Game of Thrones." We'd seen every season up until then and he bans the final one? Now THAT was cruel and unusual punishment. But I have to say this about Roberson; my personal feelings about the man aside, he was a leader. There was absolutely no question about who was in charge when he was on location. The same cannot be said for all wardens.

Warden is a very transitory position. They are constantly coming and going, while the prison's other high-ranking staff members (shift commanders, majors, senior lieutenants, Internal Affairs staff) are permanent fixtures of the institutions where they work. The permanent fixtures don't always appreciate a new warden coming in and telling them how to run their prison, especially when they feel the new warden will only be there from three to six months, which seems to be the average tenure of wardens in lower security facilities.

If you have a weak warden, as many of them are, the permanent fixtures will run them over. A typical scene with a weak warden might play out:

Warden Pussymyer (soft voice):

"I was hoping that we might be able to start an art program for the prisoners."

Major Pain/Shift Commander (loud and aggressive):

"We don't do that here, warden!"

Warden Pussymyer (jumping, startled):

"Oh! Oh, okay. I understand. I understand. Carry on, gentlemen."

The same scene with a strong warden like Roberson might play out a little differently:

Warden Roberson (assertive voice):

"We're going to start an art program here for the prisoners."

Major Pain/Shift Commander (loud and aggressive):

"We don't do that here, warden!"

Warden Roberson (taking a step closer to the major):

"I'm not interested in your opinion, major, I'm telling you what's happening. We ARE starting an art program. Make it happen."

Major Pain/Shift Commander:

"Okay, warden. I understand. I understand."

Warden Roberson:

"Carry on, gentlemen."

I didn't like Roberson. A lot of people didn't. But they respected him. You can't be a leader and worry about making the people you intend to lead angry. It doesn't work that way.

Because of Warden Roberson's support, the peer mentor training went on despite some of the staff's misgivings.

"They're doing what? Inmates leading inmates? That's crazy, it'll never work. I give it a week," said some of the less confident officers.

Other officers thought it was a good idea. Our program coordinator was an energetic young lady named Rochelle Briney. She was all in on the program. We went to the classroom five days a week to train, getting used to speaking in front of a group, becoming familiar with the material we were going to facilitate. We had to split the group in two because of social distancing concerns. Nine of us would come in the morning, eight in the afternoon. Masks were mandatory but we were getting it done.

I'd earned my certification as a Peer Educator from the Illinois Board of Public Health in 2015 when I was at Danville. Or was it Department? Board of Public Health, Department of Public Health, it was one of those. I can never remember. My point is, public speaking wasn't a big deal for me. When at Danville I'd had to do an orientation once a week before a group of prisoners new to the facility who did not want to be there and who had no interest in anything you had to say. Commanding the attention of audiences such as this is challenging, to say the least.

I was fortunate to learn from some very talented fellow peer educators, most notably Renaldo Hudson (Naldo), Joseph Mapp (Jo-Jo) and Six (can't remember his government name), among others, plus Counselor Joe Smith, who had talked me into becoming a peer educator.

Smith would often say, jokingly, that he didn't come to work to play games; he was about changing lives. Jokingly or not, he really did change my life.

My first time in front of a class did not go great. My face turned beet red. I broke out in a sweat and I was a st-st-stuttering, stammering mess. After the sink-or-swim, trial-by-fire training I'd received in Danville, and the tricks of the trade I'd picked up watching Six, Jo-Jo, and Naldo, today you could put me in front of a crowd at a football stadium and I'd be totes comfortable talking about any subject whatsoever. This is a valuable strength and life skill to have, and I owe it to Joe Smith.

The peer mentor training at Jacksonville was cake. The training consisted of us speaking in front of each other, a class of nine who were speaker-friendly. I didn't understand how anyone could be nervous. I was like the old guy in the room saying, "Back in my day…"

"When I was in Danville," I said, "I had to speak in front of a hundred convicted murderers at a time. And they all had shanks. And they all wanted to kill me! Why are you nervous?"

The training went on despite our dismal everyday life. I hope I'm accurately conveying the degree of desperation and uncertainty hanging over us throughout all this. As a writer I want to get that part right. Let's just look at one aspect. The impact of having our visits taken cannot be overstated. Men and women in prison live for visits. They are a tangible, concrete reminder that not only is there a real world out there beyond these gates, but in that world there are people there who love us.

For some of us, we threw ourselves into the peer mentor training despite the hardships of the quarantine. For others, we threw ourselves into it *because* of the hardships of the pandemic.

It gave us something to focus on other than our misery.

PRISON WAR STORIES

One of the most difficult hardships of the quarantine was the suspension of visits. Visits are extremely important to prisoners, as I'm sure you can imagine. But not every person has someone to visit them. Or maybe they have family, but no romantic interests. Or maybe they do, and they're just greedy for more.

My point is that prisoners set each other up with hookups all the time. Such was the case with my homie, Li'l D. Li'l D had a confusing name because "D" was a nickname typically associated with an organization that may or may not rhyme with the phrase Prankster Insightfuls. Li'l D, however, was a member of an organization that may or may not have rhymed with the phrase Spice Boards. As in, Totally Strong Spice Boards. Get it? Sorry, general public, I have to hold down a couple of inside jokes with my incarcerated brethren. Li'l D was from the Englewood neighborhood of Chicago.

Confusing name aside, Li'l D had been set up with a female. He wrote, then began to call. This went on for several weeks. They were hitting it off, but she had yet to send him a picture. That's what we in the biz call a "red flag." But it was all good, though, because she'd finally agreed to come and see him on a visit.

On the day of the visit, when his name was finally called, Li'l D practically skipped to the visiting room. He'd been waiting in tense anticipation for hours. His heart was bursting with audacious hope at the prospect of a fresh, new romance with this lovely queen who was coming to see him. Officers told him to sit at table eight.

"Your visitor will be in momentarily," they told him.

Li'l D sat down and watched the door. "At Last" by Etta James was playing in his imagination. Then she stepped through the doorway and the needle scratched the record. The music came to an abrupt stop.

Li'l D did not let disappointment show on his face. She'd come to see him, after all, and he didn't want to hurt her feelings. She was a larger gal.

"Okay," he thought. "They smokied me, but that's okay. Get to know her. Don't be petty." But then, quickly, came the afterthought, "That is strike one, though."

They hugged, sat down, and talked for awhile. Li'l D stayed open and optimistic. After a suitable amount of time had passed, for Li'l D did not want to appear too thirsty, he asked her, "You feel like getting something to eat?"

Eating vending machine food, which, compared to prison food, was five-star cuisine, was one of the main highlights of going on a visit. Only visitors could purchase vending machine cards; five bucks for the card, then as much as you wanted in $5 increments.

"Oh, I didn't bring in any money for a vending machine card," she replied. "I left my purse locked in the trunk of my car."

"That's okay," said Li'l D aloud. "We ain't got to eat." In his mind, though, it was, "Yep…there goes strike two, right there." He had skipped breakfast and lunch in anticipation of feasting at his visit.

His earlier optimism was gone. He was maintaining conversation out of courtesy at that point. She'd come up there to see him, and that counted for something. Not much, but something.

One of Li'l Ds homies was on a visit too. He noticed Li'l D wasn't eating. "Hey, fam, you hungry? We got plenty money left on this card," his friend said.

Li'l D is a proud brother. He was for sure, one THOUSAND percent, hungry. But Li'l D would have starved to death on that visit before accepting the hard-earned cash of another prisoner's family. That's just the kind of guy he is.

"Nah, man, no thank you, brother. I appreciate y'all, but you enjoy your visit."

His homie's mother pressed.

"Are you sure, baby? We ain't gonna use it all. Be a shame to let it go to waste."

"No ma'am, thank you so much. Y'all just save that for your next visit."

"Alright, young man," she replied. "Let me know if you change your mind."

Li'l D turned back to his visit. She leaned in close and said in a hushed voice, "Do you think you can ask them can I get something, though? I am kinda hungry."

Li'l D didn't hold it in this time. The whole visiting room heard him.

"Aw, hell no! There go strike three right there, girl, you out! We ain't fixing to do this right here. C/O!" he yelled, standing up. "Send me back, this visit's over!"

It can't be Romeo and Juliet every time.

Blackstone Career Institute
Est. 1890

Awards this Certificate in

Legal Assistant/Paralegal

with Distinction upon

Nicholas Joseph Chittick

who has fulfilled all the requirements prescribed by the School and is entitled
to all of the honors, rights and privileges thereunto appertaining.

In Testimony Whereof this recognition of achievement is

Given this 10th day of November 2020

President

Valerie L. Behrle B.S., M.Ed.
Director of Education

Figure 1: My mom visiting me in Graham Correctional Facility in 2018. Time catches up to us all. Her COPD was already beginning to progress into early Pulmonary Fibrosis and I didn't even know she was sick. Had I known it was to be our final visit, I would have told her how proud I was to be her son.

Figure 2: My mom visiting in Chicago around 1991. I was two years or so out of the Army and playing in multiple bands, convinced I was mere days away from superstardom.

Figure 3: Graham Vets flag pole in the center of the facility. The pillars represent the Army, Navy, Air Force, Marines, Coast Guard, and National Guard.

Figure 4: Graham Vets Membership card.

Figure 5: Our fearless leader, the ever-persistent
Rochelle Briney.

Figure 5: From left to right: My boy, David, my boy John, and my
sister Jenny. This was taken at Universal Studios Orlando in 2001. This is
what prisoners have to deal with; we're rotting away in prison while our
families are out there living it up! My advice is…don't go to prison.

Figure 7: My niece, Shamekia.

Figure 8: My boy Walt and his girl, Shamekia.

Figure 9: Joshua "Chavi" Chavez...Do I want a tray? DO I WANT A FUCKING TRAY!?

Figure 10: My boy Thanos...I mean The Big Hurt...no, it's Nelly. I told you...impending danger.

Figure 11: My brother Josh, Melissa McBride, and my mother at
Comi-Con a few years back.

Figure 12: My boy, Hustle.

Figure 12: My boy, Hustle, with his
mom.

CHAPTER SIXTEEN

Pandemic 1st Quarter

Lack of visitation wasn't our only hardship. Hardships came both plentiful and in many forms throughout quarantine. We weren't allowed to work out. Sure, we were allowed to go to the yard for a half-hour twice a week (thanks to JHA) but they'd removed all the weights from the iron pile. They removed all the soccer balls and basketballs, closed the handball courts, and instituted a policy of issuing an IDR to anyone who dared play any kind of sports.

They wouldn't even let us use the chin-up bars, and after they saw us working out with the picnic tables they removed those from the yard, as well. Under even the most ideal of circumstances prisoners spend inordinate amounts of time confined to stationary positions. Working out and playing sports not only functioned as a cathartic emotional release valve, it is a very necessary way in which prisoners maintain health and stave off maladies that plague those who lead a sedentary lifestyle, which was all the more important during those restrictive conditions imposed by COVID.

There was a sort of vindictiveness to the yard policies, almost as though the administration were saying, "We gotta give 'em yard, but nobody said anything about letting them work out!"

"So just what are we supposed to do out there on the yard, anyway?" one prisoner asked a C/O.

"Walk? Sit there?" the office replied. "I don't care. Our staff gym is open, so at least I still get to work out. Fuck you guys."

After this someone filed a grievance stating how the gyms in the free world had been closed, the inmate weights had been taken, so then why was the staff gym still open? It worked. Much to the extreme aggravation of Jacksonville staff, this grievance got the staff gym shut down. Man, were they pissed. It got personal after that.

Some officers started enforcing the no-working-out-in-the-day-room policy. Technically, it *was* a rule, but up until then they'd been overlooking it because we were living under extraordinary circumstances. It was also a rule that prisoners weren't supposed to get haircuts on the deck, but the barber shop was closed until further notice. If we didn't get haircuts on the deck, we didn't get haircuts. It was either get a haircut and face a possible IDR or grow your hair out and be charged five dollars for a new ID for the crime of "changing your appearance." You were breaking a rule no matter what you did.

In lieu of weights, prisoners came up with alternatives. Filling up laundry bags with books was one option. If you filled empty pop bottles or detergent containers with water, then placed an equal amount in two laundry bags to ensure equal weight, you could take a mop handle or a broomstick and you had yourself a curl bar or a bench press bar. It wasn't the same as iron, but it was better than nothing. As I've said, prisoners are nothing if not resourceful.

These weight bags became targets. Even though the rules weren't being enforced, strictly speaking, it was open season on the confiscation of weight bags. I guess some of the officers figured if they couldn't work out, then we shouldn't be able to either. They'd take our weight bags, we'd make more, they'd take them again, and we'd make more again. It became a cycle of life.

We came up with clever ways to hide them. They rarely looked in the showers or the toilet stalls. Propped open doors made a good spot that they rarely checked. It became a giant shell game. The officers would go into a room to search it, tear through it, then move on to the next room. As the guards focused their attention on searching the second room we would quietly and deftly move all of the weight bags into the room they'd already searched. Real life cat and mouse.

The peer mentor program remained a ray of light in an otherwise dismal situation. Preparations continued, despite our having lost one of our foremost supporters; Warden Roberson had been transferred to Lincoln Correctional Center. I told you, the position of warden is very transitory. His replacement was Warden Gregg Scott, the epitome of a weak warden. He wasn't a bad leader because he made bad decisions; he was a bad leader because he made *zero* decisions. His standard operating procedure was to not make waves.

Still, the program rolled on. We were allowed to name it ourselves. I don't remember who came up with what exactly, but someone had said "Level Up," and someone else had said "Better Than Before." Those were the two frontrunners. There were other names, all bad. We collectively settled on, "LEVEL UP: Better Than Before." Hustle and Nelly had been selected as mentors, and rightfully so. Many prisoners already looked to them as leaders.

We had B, the quintessential angry black man, volatile but a great speaker. We had Chavez, the DJ/gear head/drug dealer who'd been busted with pounds and pounds of cocaine and marijuana. He'd successfully completed my music theory class, and I'd recently finished preparing his clemency petition. Then there were Walt and I, two world-class virtuoso musicians.

We had Mo-Mo, who I'd known for 20 years and been in a few different prisons with. Cardio, Cole, and Dolla, three classic street hustlers. Reformed, of course. Our mascot, Cody, the comic relief. He was a character. We had Ricky, a gym-rat white boy who was always preoccupied with whether or not he had enough definition in this or that muscle group. Chavez was like that too, they were a couple of mirror gazers. They worked out a lot together now that I think about it. We had our number one brother like no other, Mr. Brian Abel, who we called Unstable Abel. He had anger management and other minor mental and emotional problems. Then there was T.Y., the smooth operator who was always writing a different female every night of the week. We had DeBerry, the hustling Mr. In-Between family man/criminal who was ready to finally go legit. Nelly had nicknamed him DeBelly because of his protruding stomach.

My mom always told me if you don't have something nice to say about someone, don't say anything at all. Finally, we had Count and Buddha, they…

Anyway, we had a decent squad for the most part. Local media wanted to do an interview with our program coordinator Rochelle Briney and two of the mentors. Nelly and I were selected to represent the program at the interview. It appeared in the August 3, 2020 issue of the "Jacksonville Courier."

None of us knew it at the time, but even then there was already dissention and discord brewing behind the scenes concerning our program. The counselors at Jacksonville did not like the social workers. Our program coordinator, Rochelle Briney, was a social worker.

As I've stated earlier, I was the clerk in Clinical Services in Danville for three years. There the social workers and the counselors worked together like a well-oiled machine. They were consummate professionals who got sh…stuff done. Under Head Counselor Jamie Tate they were a force united.

Clinical Services in Jacksonville was something else entirely. The head counselor there was a man named Van Winkle, but he was in charge in title only. The real control and authority was in the hands of a regular counselor named Ms. Delaney. She was in a relationship with a certain union president, which she used to her advantage. She would bring heat on anyone who defied her through her connections, and though there were many who did not personally like her, they had to "play nice" with her because of who she was sleeping with. Straight soap opera.

The counselors and social workers in Jacksonville did not even share the same office space, which was completely out of the ordinary; their offices were not even in the same building. In fact, their officers were located in the two furthermost buildings from one another than any two other buildings on the grounds. The nature of the enmity between social worker and counselor resembled high school…wait. No, check that. It resembled *grade school* clique politics. "Mean Girls," junior edition.

Social workers were highly educated with ongoing educational requirements that continued throughout their careers. They underwent years of training in order to obtain qualifications to teach classes and conduct various group sessions. Anyone with a GED could be a counselor, on the other hand, and it seemed that the counselors in general, and Ms. Delaney in particular, resented the social workers' qualifications.

I have a theory on why this was so. It's just a theory but see what you think. Used to be back in the day when someone hired on as a counselor they were a counselor. Hired on as a dietary supervisor, they were a dietary supervisor. Law librarians were law librarians. LTS supervisors were...you get the idea.

Somewhere along the line the guards decided to make lateral moves to the nonsecurity staff positions. Today, we have a bunch of counselors, dietary supervisors, maintenance supervisors, inmate commissary supervisors, and others who wear that title, but in their hearts they are still security. Nothing but a bunch of guards in charge of everything. In fact, a common slam you might hear against a counselor or dietary supervisor from a coworker might be, "Your opinion doesn't count, you never even worked in security."

There is a certain mentality that some guards have. Once they have it, they never lose it. Not all guards have this mentality, and for the ones that do, they have it in varying degrees of intensity. But in a nutshell this mentality is; prisoners are not people. They don't love their children like we do. They're all liars, animals, and scumbags. I call it the Nancy Grace Delusion. They point to us and say, "There goes the bad guy!" What does that make them? Good? You caught me, that last part is from "Scarface." Still, it's apt.

Many staff members at Jacksonville proved through their actions every day that they deeply believed in this mindset. People like Van Winkle, Delaney, Ashley Clement (the Healthcare Unit Administrator, true Wexford through and through), Dietary Superintendent White, Dietary Supervisor Beckman, a whole host of others, true pieces of shit, one and all. In fairness to the other staff there, though, I feel I have to say that a lot of them were just hardworking blue-collar guys and gals who came to work and did their jobs without taking joy in torturing prisoners with petty vindictiveness. People like Edwards, Hartley, Getz,

Sgt. Murphy, Pat, Collins, Rentschler, Briney, Moeller, Savco, Boyd, Dahl, Schroeder, and many others. Decent human beings who treated people with respect until that person gave them a reason not to.

All the behind-the-scenes politics aside, Level Up: Better Than Before was set to launch. We were starting with nine different groups; Anger Management, Effective Communication, Conflict Resolution, Life Skills, Building Resiliency, Mindfulness, Change & Success, and Coping with Negativity. The cycles would be 10 weeks with each participant (or mentee) required to sign up for four groups. Four hours of group per week. We would add more in later cycles, but this was the itinerary for our maiden voyage.

Mentors would function in two-man teams. To fairly divide the workload and desirable time slots between us we came up with the idea of selecting them via draft, as with a Fantasy Football League. Partners were selected and a draft was conducted. After some last-minute changes in the lineup due to creative differences, I ended up with Chavez as a partner. I was cool with it. We would be moving to B Wing of Housing Unit 1, this was going to be our program deck. A mere hop across the hall for Nelly, Hustle, Chavez, and myself. Convenient.

As we were preparing ourselves for the move, on one of my last nights in Room 4 I received legal mail again. I was not so naïve and foolishly optimistic as before. I signed for it, then opened it with stoic resignation. Due to my inability to pay the filing fee Judge Myerscough was dismissing my case *without prejudice*. This meant that I could refile it at a later time so long as the statute of limitations had not passed. I wasn't surprised. During my ordeal in Graham I'd often wondered how they could act so brazenly with total deliberate indifference to my medical needs. Here was my answer; the deck was completely stacked against prisoners.

I wasn't sure whether I'd refile. I was pretty disheartened. Between my overall low morale, the quarantine, my health issues, the constant pain I was in, my worry over my mother's health, the demands of helping to create and implement Level Up, the energy I was investing in my Blackstone studies, the demands of my daily grind as a co-called jailhouse lawyer (I was still practicing) helping others who needed this or that motion, petition, or letter typed up, and yes…the sting of this courtroom loss over a trivial formality that should have been a slam dunk

(I was better than this; it was like Steph Curry shooting an air ball at the buzzer), between all this and the general drain of being in prison I didn't have anything left to put into preparing a new pleading.

I got an email from my mom on June 22, 2020. She was being checked into an Orlando, Florida area hospital on Monday, June 22. She'd sent the email the day before, on Sunday, but I didn't get it until the following day. Our emails are delayed for screening. She was about to undergo the extensive preparations necessary for a lung transplant. She didn't have my prison email app on her phone, only her computer, so there'd be no more email until she came home. Also, I didn't have her cell on my approved list, only her land line. I submitted her cell for approval, but that would take at least three weeks for it to be processed. I should have called her the night before. If I'd received the email when she'd sent it, I would have. I'd talked to her once or twice a week for the past 20 years and had been emailing her once a week since 2018 when prison emails became a thing. Who knew when I'd speak to her again? More uncharted territory. 2020 had plenty of that.

I had no way of knowing this when I read it, but that email was the last one I would ever receive from her.

Chapter Seventeen

Pandemic 2nd Quarter

We were moving into a new era. It was our last night in Room 4 prior to the massive upheaval that was going to occur in the morning when they cleared out B Wing and began moving the Level Up people there. Everyone knew that monumental change was going to occur on the morrow.

Therefore, as could be expected, shit went haywire that night.

An A Wing tradition that had started during the quarantine was the practice of room wars. The occupants of one room might rush into another room and begin beating up those unlucky enough to be caught unaware. Surprise attack! Got to stay ready. Not really fighting to injure, but arm shots, leg shots, and body blows. The pain was real.

Or several of another room's inhabitants might fall upon a lone occupant of a rival room as he was in the dayroom or hallway, seizing him, lifting him up, and taking him into a random room, then plunking him down into a random top bunk whether it were his or not, and sometimes whether that bunk was occupied or not.

"You're about to get some company!" Plop, down he goes onto the bunk next to some random unsuspecting dude.

Someone talking smack to another person might say, "Keep talking crazy, we're gonna wrap your ass up and put you in the top bunk."

Any time Room 4 got rushed we dealt with our foes in an orderly fashion. Nelly, Hustle, Snoody, Too-Tall, Simeon, Uncle Drew, Cutty, Vok, even old man Johnny and the rest, we had a squad. We were undefeated. My old crippled ass was less than useless, but I was there for moral support and a couple cheap shots if someone was already being held down.

On the eve of the mass move it was utter pandemonium. Rampant room wars all night.

Room 4 remained undefeated.

We moved en masse the following morning, a chaotic exodus. They did half of us one day, then the other half the next. The 17 mentors were moved into the same room, Room 10. Walt moved over from Housing Unit 2 and became my neighbor, moving into the bunk next to mine. Two of our open top bunks in Room 10 were used for bookshelves, we stored all of our facilitation materials there. We also stored 12 plastic chairs for groups. We knew that if we left them unattended in the dayroom they'd end up everywhere. A desk was placed in the dayroom. Three dry erase boards were installed.

We'd been preparing to initiate our program for several weeks. We'd even participated in an interview with local media. To show the extent of the lack of communication between staff, every day at least one officer, sergeant, or lieutenant would step onto the deck and say, "What is this, some kind of honor dorm or something?"

Or they would look in Room 10 and say, "What are these chairs and books doing in here? Get this stuff out of here."

"Whoa, Lou, this is the Level Up Program. We have authorization to have this stuff in here."

"What the hell is Level Up?"

It happened again and again and again. You'd think they might discuss it at roll call. These were the early indications that not everyone (cough, cough...Delaney, Van Winkle...cough, cough) was on board with Level Up.

In the draft, Chavez and I had drawn Anger Management, Effective Communication, Building Resiliency, and Mindfulness. He was a little nervous about facilitating, but this actually worked in his favor. His aversion to public speaking was a motivating factor in his class preparations; he knew the material inside and out and had a game plan at every group. He converted his weakness into a strength.

The whole point of the peer mentored group idea was that participation in Level Up wasn't going to magically make you a better person. Anger Management wasn't going to magically make you someone who no longer got angry. What it did was if you *wanted* to learn to control your anger, Anger Management *would* provide you with the tools to do so. If you *wanted* to stay out of prison when you got out, Level Up and the groups we facilitated *could* provide you with some tools and practices that would help you be able to do so. But you had to want it. You had to do the work for yourself.

The program was off and running, though. We had rendered our vision a reality, just as the guys on the Building Block in Danville had done before us. Level Up, in fact, was the only programming that continued through quarantine. Everything else was suspended, but Ms. Briney would attend our sessions in full PPE gear, taking notes and working out the bugs. Even the GEO Group Drug Program was suspended.

Personally—and this is just my opinion, I'm not stating this as a fact—I believe that GEO Group is the biggest scam going in American corrections today. I recently read in "Prison Legal News" that they just signed another $700 million contract somewhere. They're a monster.

I don't know, maybe GEO programs do help some prisoners, somewhere, but certainly not the way they were conducted in Jacksonville. There, GEO was one thing and one thing only; a way that prisoners could earn good conduct credits and get out sooner. I don't know whether it did anything to help them with their substance abuse and other issues, but it definitely got them out of prison sooner so they get back to their meth/crack/heroin/whatever earlier. I know the guys who vied for slots in the GEO Drug Program and I heard their conversations. I witnessed them come back to prison. The earlier in the spring they got out, the sooner in the summer they could come back to prison.

For a program to be a success you have to select participants who are serious about their desire to change. GEO's only requirement was "Can you earn GCC (good conduct credits)? If so, come on and we'll sign you up." I fail to see how GEO's three-hour group sessions, which consisted of participants reading and commenting on essays about following the rules while a disinterested counselor leafed through an issue of "Better Homes and Gardens," prepared guys for release.

And another thing that made no sense to me was GEO's adamant refusal to allow any participant to speak about their past. Of course, I understand the necessity of not glorifying past criminal behavior, this was common sense, but allowing no discussion about the past at all was counterproductive. You can't grow and develop without examining and analyzing the mistakes of your past. Those unfamiliar with history are doomed to repeat it.

Yet another thing about GEO was their policy of encouraging participants to snitch on one another, often for the most minor of infractions. They called it a "Pull Up," but petty snitchery was all it was. I didn't see how ratting out your neighbor for leaving his TV on while he went to take a piss helped anyone overcome their addiction or stay out of prison, but then again, I don't think GEO was particularly concerned with reducing recidivism. Why would they want to prevent their primary source of income from returning to the marketplace?

Level Up: Better Than Before participants could not earn good conduct credits for participation in our program. We couldn't get them out sooner, but then again, that was not our goal.

We were more concerned with making sure that once they got out of prison, they *stayed* out of prison.

CHAPTER EIGHTEEN

Pandemic 2nd Quarter

When July 15th came I tried calling my mom's cell, but the number was not yet approved. I knew she was in the hospital, I'd spoken to my dad at the house, but it'd been more than three weeks since last we spoke. I'd actually had Walt do a three-way phone call when he'd still been over in Housing Unit 2 (very much against the rules) to check on her for me. He called Sham…someone and had them dial my mom's cell. She relayed the message that she was fine, thank God.

Wait. I remembered that wrong. What I *meant* to say, according to my team of legal advisors, was that I had Walt call Sham…someone, who then, after talking to Walt, called and checked on my mother in such a way that no IDOC rules or regulations were broken at any time. There. For anyone in authority who may someday read this, that's how it really happened.

Anyway, my mother's cell should have been on my list of approved numbers by then, but it wasn't. I didn't know it yet, but Securus (the IDOC's telecommunications contractor) had messed up the paperwork, thereby obliterating any opportunity I had for some final conversations with her. It took several weeks, usually, to resolve a phone issue. Phone issues were common, they had their own special form to fill out. The form was entitled "Phone Issues." It was too bad it usually took several weeks to resolve a phone issue. My mom was several weeks from passing away.

Level Up's first couple of weeks passed by. There were a few wrinkles to iron out, but we'd gotten the kite off the ground and into the air, so to speak. One morning the Illinois National Guard came onto the grounds. We all stared out the windows. What the hell were they doing out there? They installed medical quarantine tents in the gym, as it turned out. It was a prophetic move because the first week of August the C/Os and other staff began coming to work in full PPE gear; hair nets, booties, gowns, gloves, masks, and face shields. We went back on total quarantine, no patio, no yard, no chow hall, no anything. It was our third week of the program, going into week four. What part of the game was this? Did they know something we didn't know? Was coronavirus at our doorstep?

Then people began getting sick. Uh oh. It was going down like a brown clown in a nightgown. It was for real, for real, now. The situation was sketch.

Information came trickling in. Not all at once, but in bits and pieces. Here's what we knew. Officer Patty had recently retired. There was a mandate from Rob Jeffreys (the Director of the IDOC) to his employees to restrict their contact with the general public to essential travel only inasmuch as it was possible to do so. There was also a similar mandate from Governor Pritzker. Despite these mandates, C/O Patty decided to have her retirement party anyway. Who knows, maybe she had a good reason. Maybe she'd already put a deposit down on the kegs.

In any event, about 30 Jacksonville staff allegedly attended this party. In addition to this, it was reported in print media (I read the article myself) that there was allegedly no one wearing masks and no social distancing at this party. Multiple staff members became infected at this party and allegedly brought COVID into the facility. Some staff were reportedly aware they were symptomatic yet came to work anyway.

Once COVID got into the facility it spread like wildfire. Only a few days after staff began wearing PPE, every man in Housing Unit 1 had coronavirus. Every last one of us. Walt and I realized it one day when he made cheeseburgers. He rarely cooked, but when he did he went all out. Walt's one of those guys who's great at whatever he does. It's slightly annoying, if I'm being honest, but his cooking game was on point. He loaded the burgers with onions, peppers, bacon, cheese, BBQ sauce, pickles, and other stuff. He handed me one and I took a bite. Why did it taste so bland?

"You put jalapenos on these?" I asked.

"Yeah," Walt replied. He took a bite. "These don't taste like anything."

We had lost our sense of taste and smell. We had COVID.

"Well," said Walt, "...this was a big waste of money."

Mo-Mo was the first to go to the quarantine tents. As a way to screen for the virus the nurses began taking our temperatures three times a day. The only way to get a COVID test was to have a fever. It was a stupid way to do it because every one of us (100 percent) had the virus, but very few of us ever had fevers. Some of us were asymptomatic, others had mild symptoms, and still others were hit hard.

Nelly was one of those who were hit hard. He stayed in his bunk for three days barely eating or drinking. It was jarring to see this person whom I'd come to perceive as invincible so incapacitated. Nelly was messed up something decent. He was the next to go to the quarantine tents.

The quarantine tents filled up quickly. The administration realized that they had to do something. One thing that had happened during quarantine was that all transfers had ceased. No prisons had any new prisoners coming in. Even though transfers had stopped, however, there were still prisoners going home every day. Jacksonville was bleeding inmates. With our numbers now well below 800 (from 1,000), they had room to clear out Housing Unit 2 and designate it as COVID Housing. For the way they treated the people who went there, it may as well have been a leper colony.

It didn't make any sense, anyway. The whole idea of moving us around from one house to another was asinine because every single one of us already had COVID before they ever moved the first guy to the quarantine tents.

"You know we all have COVID already, right?" I said to a nurse taking our temperature. "What's the point in taking our temperature three times a day?"

"You don't have COVID unless we say you have COVID," she replied.

Here's how I got caught up and sent to quarantine. Now, this next part is pretty embarrassing for me, but here goes. Among my myriad health issues, gastric motility and blood in my stool was among them. Food was not moving through my system, basically. It was likely related to my spinal damage, but they were sending me out for a colonoscopy.

Yes, they were going to jam a camera up my ass, alright? It's a legitimate medical procedure, so can we be adults about this? Oh, is that funny to you? A penis-like camera taking Polaroids of my hemorrhoids, and YOU think that's FUNNY? How dare you! I got a three-foot cable gonna be snaked up my mud dragon stable, and you're sitting there laughing! Realll mature. What's wrong with you? A man getting a giant piece of dildo-shaped gadgetry rammed up his fudge factory is NOT funny, so STOP LAUGHING! Jerks.

Anyway…I was having a colonoscopy. They took me to the Healthcare Unit and gave me a COVID test, the one where they acted like they were trying to scrape childhood memories out of your brain. It sucked.

"You know this test is going to come back positive, right?" I said to the nurse administering the test.

"Why do you say that?" she asked.

"Because I'm in house one, and every single one of us over there have coronavirus," I replied.

"Why do all you guys keep saying that? You're not doctors."

"C'mon, we sleep one foot away from each other and share five sinks between a hundred of us. You're a professional healthcare worker, Li'l Miss Essential," I said. She was wearing a t-shirt that said ESSENTIAL, I guess for essential worker. "You understand how airborne viruses work. I bet you a thousand dollars this test comes back positive."

"Then how come you don't have a fever, smart guy?"

"Because obviously a fever has very little to do with coronavirus. It's definitely a piss-poor indicator because less than 10 of the guys had a fever and all of us have coronavirus."

"Wow. You should have been a doctor for the CDC," she said sarcastically.

"I know," I replied sincerely. "I would have been great."

Sparring with staff like that is fun sometimes. The Jacksonville nurses didn't have the same mean spiritedness as the ones in Graham.

The reason for my COVID test was so that if I tested negative I'd be isolated for 72 hours, then sent out on my procedure. It was COVID protocol. But that's not what happened. My test, just as I had predicted, came back positive.

I was in my isolation cell in the healthcare unit. It was about 11:30 pm. I was lying on my bunk playing solitaire on my tablet when an officer placed his back against my door, then mule kicked it as hard as he could four times in a row. I damn near dropped my tablet, the ignorant son of a bitch had startled me so bad.

"Pack your shit and go to Housing Unit 2!" he yelled. "You're not going on your furlough, you've got COVID!"

It was a hell of a way for me to find out. I could have made an issue about him, nonmedical staff, informing me of my medical status. It was a HIPAA violation like a mo fo, but whatever. We were in difficult times, no sense in being a jerk about it. I didn't have the energy to be a jerk, anyway, even if I'd wanted to.

No nurses spoke to me or offered any medication, instructions, or education on what to expect from my illness. I took my overnight bag to Housing Unit 1 where the remainder of my personal property sat unattended on a cart outside. Lucky it wasn't raining out. I grabbed the cart and pushed it to Housing Unit 2.

I was told by the C/O at the desk that I was being moved into 10-17. That was a top bunk.

"I have a bottom bunk permit," I said. "I had a spinal injury a couple of years back."

"I don't give a fuck what you had," he replied. "We don't have any bottom bunks open, not on B Wing. A Wing is empty, we're not gonna open it up just so you can have a bottom bunk."

"We'll see about that," I thought to myself, but did not say.

I moved my stuff into B Wing and took my property to the corner, setting up shop right there on the dayroom floor like a homeless guy in a Chicago alleyway. I saw Mo-Mo. Nelly was somewhere on location laid up in his bunk. COVID was kicking his ass. There were two black nurses in the bubble I'd never seen before. They weren't part of the Jacksonville roster. I had a banging headache, so I poked my head out to see if they had any ibuprofen. I barely got the words out when she snapped at me.

"We're not here to give you medicine or medical attention or answer questions about COVID or anything else. We're here to take your vitals, that's it. There's no reason for any of you to talk to us, so tell your friends."

"Did you ever used to work in Graham?" I asked.

"Go," said the C/O, pointing to the door.

Fine, be that way.

I went back to my mattress on the floor in the corner, surrounded by my TV, typewriter, fan, and property boxes. At a little after midnight another prisoner came in with his property. He made it a few steps onto the deck when he saw me.

"What the hell are you doing?" he asked. My place on the dayroom floor was not something one saw every day.

"They're trying to make me go in a top bunk, but I have a bottom bunk permit," I said.

"Me too!" he replied.

"Plenty of room over here," I said, looking for a rappie.

He set up shop as well a few feet away. A little while later another prisoner came. His attention was drawn to us as soon as he stepped onto the deck.

"What's your guys' deal?" he asked.

"We have bottom bunk permits, but they're trying to make us go in top bunks," said my new rappie.

"I just told dude's ass out there, I'm too sick to be getting in and out of a top bunk. I ain't got no bottom bunk permit, but still."

"We got space," I said.

By 3 am there were five of us. We were stretched out like a cluster of homeless guys under an overpass. All that was missing was a fire. A lieutenant walked onto the deck shortly after three o'clock. He made it about three steps into the wing when he noticed us all.

"Okay. What in the fuck are you guys doing on the floor out here in the dayroom?" he asked.

"I have a bottom bunk permit," I said.

"So do I," said the other guy.

"I'm too sick to be climbing into a top bunk," said another.

The lieutenant reversed course, cracked open the door, and spoke to the officer.

"You want to step in here for a second?" The guard came in and the lieutenant motioned to us. "Care to explain?"

"Get to your bunks, NOW!" yelled the guard. He was angry because we were making him look bad in front of his boss.

"Two of these guys say they have bottom bunk orders," said the lieutenant.

"We don't have any bottom bunks open on this side, Lou," said the officer.

"How long have you guys been out here?" the lieutenant asked us.

"I got here around midnight," I replied.

"These guys have been out here on the floor for three hours?"

The officer didn't respond.

"Let me talk to you out here," he said to the C/O.

A natural reaction, all the prisoners made that collective "oooohhhhh" sound, like when one of your classmates gets called to the principal's office.

"Shut up!" the lieutenant snapped at us, his face stern. He was not amused.

All of us were moved across the hall to A Wing, and each of us were given bottom bunks. I've rarely seen a more angry C/O. The inside of his face shield was fogged up and everything.

I was placed in a room by myself. Me and 19 empty bunks. It was very eerie. COVID already had me feeling out of it, but alone in that room, that night, I felt the presence of something. Things, hidden but there, malevolent, just out of sight, like slithering creatures of the swamp that remain safely below the water line, the only evidence of their existence the slight ripples on the surface caused by their covert movements underneath. That's what I saw. Ripples on the surface of reality. Or maybe it was just COVID messing with my mind. Either way, I had the heebie jeebies.

I'd had eerie feelings in prison before. For awhile in Cook County Jail I went through some issues with my mental health. I became convinced that I'd been killed in my drug deal gone bad, that I was dead. I wasn't in jail, not really. Instead, I was in hell. Or maybe purgatory, but I and all the other people in the jail were definitely dead and didn't know it. Took me awhile to break out of that one.

In Menard I saw someone walk past the bars of my cell one night, out on the gallery, I clearly saw them out of my peripheral vision.

"Who in the hell is out and about at this hour?" I thought to myself.

When I put my mirror out of the bars to see who it was there was no one there. This happened more than once.

When I transferred to Galesburg from Menard I was ordered to walk to personal property to claim my belongings. Menard had been maximum security, which meant that prisoners were escorted by a guard everywhere they went. I spent six-and-a-half years in Menard. In Galesburg that evening it was about 6 pm, right around dusk. I went to the exit and waited. After about 15 minutes an officer came walking around the corner. He stopped short when he saw me.

"What the hell are you waiting for?" he asked.

"My escort," I replied. He laughed.

"Where'd you come here from, Stateville or Menard?" he asked.

"Menard," I said.

"Yeah, man, I thought so. You're not in a max joint anymore, you don't need to be escorted here. Just walk over to property, they're waiting for you."

"Are you sure?"

"Yeah," he said, amused by my hesitation. "It's fine."

I stepped cautiously outside. It was just getting dark, the sun already sunken below the horizon where orange and purple blended across the sky, bleeding into dark blue, and finally black on the opposite horizon. I saw Orion's belt, that familiar constellation I'd seen so many times before as a teenager night-sailing on the Indian River in Cocoa Beach, Florida, or sometimes the Banana River, back when my life lay ahead as open as the water I sailed on, my future bristling with hope and possibility.

Seeing that familiar constellation in that Illinois sky in 2007 as I walked to property, it wasn't hope I felt, but trepidation. A scene from, "The Shawshank Redemption," played vividly in my imagination, the part where Warden Norton lures Tommy Williams out into the courtyard to have him murdered. I was convinced I was about to die. Not another soul was stirring anywhere on the grounds. I walked a zig-zag pattern on the sidewalk. I know any guards watching me from the towers had to be thinking to themselves, "What the heck is this guy doing?" I waited for the shot to ring out, but it never came.

Being in that empty room in Jacksonville brought on similar feelings of trepidation. It was like being inside an episode of "The Walking Dead," it was that creepy. Scooby-Doo, where are you? You have to understand, it was totally unprecedented. I'd spent the entire past 20-plus years in overcrowded conditions. There was an actual *echo* in the room. I made it to sleep sometime just before sunrise, but those COVID dreams were disturbing, to say the least. I awoke several hours later, the room awash in daylight, my head pounding like a jackhammer. No medication was offered, save for two occasions when they brought a single dose of ibuprofen to every prisoner. But it didn't happen while I was in Housing Unit 2. The so-called COVID House was a straight-up horror show. If you got really, really sick they might take you to the quarantine tents where you might receive some imitation of medical attention, maybe. All they did where we were at was take your temperature and vitals three times a day, waking you up in the middle of the night one of those times to do it.

My second day there I looked across the hall and saw Walt. On the one hand, I was glad to have a brother to go through the BS with, but on the other, I was bummed my friend had to go through this BS. I wouldn't wish it on anyone. Quarantine was especially hard on Walt and others like him. People with money. Here's why; Walt rarely ate in the chow hall, and I'm talking once or twice a month, if that. I believe it's one of the reasons he was still so healthy after so many years in prison. The IDOC website will tell you that, "...the Department provides each of its offenders with a nutritional diet in accordance with blah, blah, blah." Yeah, right. Chow hall food will kill you. Farm-feed-grade soy, undercooked, processed turkey/chicken loaf, and food prepared in unsanitary conditions by cooks who had no idea what they were doing, often supervised by people who had even less of an idea what they were doing. That was Jacksonville's kitchen under White's supervision.

The food in Graham had been excellent by comparison, just to be fair to the IDOC.

On quarantine, however, spending limits had been set at the inmate commissary, capped at $30 per week. Commissary was much more expensive than grocery store food. You can't live on $30 worth of food a week. It's impossible. Walt had to start eating chow hall food. I've known him for many years, it was totally out of his character. It was like seeing a lion eating a salad. What the…?

Our wing was empty, there were only five of us. There was an old man among us…older than even me, I mean. He was coughing, wheezing and moaning, crying out for help. "God help me! I'm dying! I'm dying!" It sounded as though he were fighting for every breath. The nurses and C/Os ignored him.

I'm a relatively compassionate person, especially by prison standards. I'll fight if I'm forced to, I have many times, but I don't enjoy conflict or take pleasure in hurting people. I've been called soft, weak, scary, and all that because of it, but whatever. I have no fear of physical pain, my threshold for pain is through the roof, but I don't like to see people suffer. I suppose the musician in me wants everything to be in tune. Strife is not harmonious.

A couple guys were laughing at the old man's distress. I didn't see anything funny about it. I felt they should help him, and I felt powerless to do anything about it. I had words with one of the C/Os about it, one of the ones from the work camp.

"What do you want me to do about it, I'm not a doctor," he said.

After the sixth or seventh straight hour of hearing the old man moan, however, my compassion wore pretty thin. I was messed up too, I had a damaged spinal cord and all the maladies that came with it, plus I had COVID too, and you didn't hear me whining about it. After so many hours I finally reached my breaking point. I screamed out, "IF YOU'RE DYING, THEN GO ON AND DIE ALREADY! BUT WHATEVER YOU DO, SHUT…THE FUCK…UP!"

I felt bad after I said it. I stopped feeling bad when he kept moaning.

It didn't take long for our wing to fill up. After the first couple days of emptiness, they started bringing in people by the hour. After a week we were nearly at capacity. They moved a bunch of guys on CPAP machines into my room, overflow from the quarantine tents. The constant beeping and whirring of their machines was like living in a sleep deprivation chamber. I had a hard time sleeping even under ideal conditions, let alone this circus atmosphere.

The deck became filthy and nasty; everyone was sick, and no one was cleaning. Nearly a hundred men not cleaning up after themselves in the shower, at the sinks, in the dayroom. Guards pushed food carts onto the wing and let us fend for ourselves. Oversleep, don't eat. There was no structure or guidance. We didn't go outside. We didn't do anything. It was a warehouse of flesh where we simply existed from one day to the next.

It wasn't Disneyland, not by a long shot.

CHAPTER NINETEEN

Pandemic 2nd Quarter

August 15 came and went, I tried my mom's cell number again. It still wasn't approved. I wrote a request slip to Clinical Services, to Ms. Sumpter, our GTL/Securus Liaison. I received a response back stating that my mom's number had been approved on July 17. I went to dial it.

"THE NUMBER YOU ARE CALLING IS NOT ON YOUR LIST OF APPROVED NUMBERS," said the automated Securus voice. What the heck?

It took a little further investigating, but here's what happened. Brevard County, Florida's area code is 321. Cook County, Illinois's area code (one of them) is 312. When the person processing the list looked at the number, they said to themselves, "Hey, this guy wrote Chicago's area code wrong. He wrote 321. Chicago is 312. Of course he meant Chicago, he's in prison in Illinois. All these guys are from Chicago! Well, we can do him a favor this one time. We'll fix it for him. He can thank us later."

I was pissed. It's always something. I wrote another request to Ms.

Sumpter asking her to troubleshoot the situation. Hopefully she could do something about it.

After a few utterly hellish weeks in COVID House, I was told I was being moved to Housing Unit 5.

"Why am I going to House 5?" I asked. "I'm in the Level Up Program."

"House 5 is for COVID recovery now," said the officer.

"COVID recovery? This doesn't make any sense. Why are they moving us around? Every man inside every housing unit in this prison has already had COVID! There ain't nobody here who hasn't had it! Not one!"

"Look, Chittick," he said. I won't use his name. "I know it. We all know it. Ashley [Clement, Jacksonville's Health Care Unit Administrator] and Doctor Baker are doing this to cover their asses. They don't want anybody to know how bad they fucked this up. They had all the time in the world to get ready, and they didn't do shit. You know it and I know it. We know the virus was already done blazing through this whole joint before they ever lifted a finger to do anything about it."

He was right. I had no choice but to move to Housing Unit 5, even if it was all just for show. The day I moved in our numbers were down to around 600. We were working our way to half capacity. Even though prisoner numbers were down, staff numbers were way up. Green County Work Camp had closed and word around the campfire was that Pittsfield Work Camp was getting ready to close next. They had already allowed the Green County Work Camp staff to come to Jacksonville so they could still get paid. Where the housing units normally had two officers to oversee them, they now had four. Work Camp dietary supervisors came to work to hang out in the kitchen offices for eight hours. There was nothing for them to do, but they had to physically be there in order to collect their paychecks. They were going to allow the Pittsfield staff to come next. And people wonder why the state of Illinois is broke.

Can you imagine something like this happening in the private sector? Ford decides to close a factory, but they tell their workers, "We're shutting this place down! But we have another factory a couple of towns over, and we're going to send you people there so you can still earn your paychecks. Now, there's nothing for you to do there, that factory is already fully staffed, but you just go there and hang out, and we're going to keep paying you." Yeah right. Only government jobs do that.

Housing Unit 5 was a total clusterfuck. After a minor detour for a day or two, I ended up on what was commonly referred to as the *old man deck*. The geezers had been sweating any staff member who'd walk by about when they would be able to return to the over-forty wing.

"When are we getting our over-forty wing back?" an old man asked Lt. Nance one time.

"Never," Lt. Nance said. "There's not going to be an old man deck anymore." Nance was only messing with them, but you should've seen their reaction.

"Wellll bullSHIT!" said one old man so forcefully his false teeth almost came flying out of his head. "We're a'getting' our deck back!"

The mob of seniors were practically shaking their canes and walkers at Nance in a display of Geezer rage. If they'd chased him out of the building it would have been one of the slowest chases in the history of chases.

When I got there I couldn't believe that this was the place these old dudes had wanted to get back to. It was a real shithole, almost as nasty as COVID House had been. The water pressure in the showers was a joke; it was like getting pissed on. Who knows, maybe that's why they liked it so much. A bunch of pervert, stinking old me, half of whom were pedophiles. If you ever wanted to do a live action version of *Family Guy*, you had about thirty candidates to audition for the role of *Herbert*. It was a far cry from Level Up. If anything, it was Level Down.

Walt made it over there, him and a few other younger guys. The geezers were all up in arms about that one, boy.

"Why's them sum bitches over here? They ain't over forty. Ain't even over thirty, seems to me. They gots to GO!"

They were pretty territorial, those geezers. As far as I was concerned, they could keep it. All I wanted was to get back to Housing Unit 1. Walt, by contrast, loved it over there. The old guys never used the phone; he could talk to Shamekia twenty times a day if he felt like it. She probably got sick of hearing his voice when he was over there, he talked to her so much. Nah, I'm kidding. Shameeks loves Walt. I'm sure it was fine. Probably.

Ms. Sumpter got my phone issue worked out and had my mom's cell processed as an emergency. I was grateful, I was finally going to call and talk to her. It'd been over two months.

She was still in the hospital, but she'd undergone all necessary preparations and was now just waiting on a donor set of lungs. I told her about the interview I'd done with the newspaper for Level Up. She told me that there was a donor shortage going on. Seems that the quarantine, ironically, because it was a policy put in place with the intention of keeping high risk people like my mom safe, was responsible for the shortage. No one was going anywhere or doing anything, so there were fewer traffic accidents and other events that led to donor organs becoming available. My mom couldn't catch her breath and had a hard time talking, so it was a short conversation. Still, it had been good to finally hear her voice.

I was very worried about her. Thoughts came unbidden into my mind. If I killed myself, could they send her my lungs? We were the same blood type, O positive. But no, she wouldn't want that.

But wait, what about a child molester? There was certainly no shortage.

"Hey," I would say to them. "You wouldn't happen to know your blood type, would you? Why do I want to know? Oh, no reason. Just making conversation. Hmm, O positive, you say? Interesting. You look like you're in pretty good shape. Do you run a lot? Oh, you do? You love cardio, set some track records in high school? Awesome, man, awesome. Say, let me talk to you for a second over here in this darkened corner."

But no, she wouldn't want that, either. Truth is, I felt totally powerless to help her, and those stupid little daydreams helped me to get through. Walt was the only one I told what was going on. I asked him to pray, and I prayed very fervently that night. It was an odd thing to pray for, if you think about it. For one family to have a miracle, another family would need to experience tragedy.

It was around seven o'clock in the evening the next day when something told me I should call my mom. I usually only used the phone once a week, and she'd had a hard time talking the day before, but still. Something told me to call, so I did. I went with my first mind. It was September 11, 2020.

My sister, Jenny, answered my mom's cell. We hadn't spoken to each other in twenty years or more.

"Hello, Nick? It's Jenny. Let me step out of the room so we can talk."

Uh-oh. This didn't bode well.

Jenny told me it wasn't looking good; one of our mom's lungs had perforated. She couldn't talk because she was intubated and was breathing with the help of machines. She mentioned that after I'd called they'd looked up my Level Up interview on her phone and mom had been very proud. I didn't care about that, though. She said that they were still holding out hope for a last minute donor to come through, but it was now a matter of hours. There was a long silence. I couldn't speak.

"Nick?" Jenny said. "Are you still there?"

"Yes."

"Are you okay?"

"No."

"I know," she said. "Listen, Mom is awake. She can't talk, but she can hear you. Do you want to say something?"

"Yes."

I wanted to say a lot. I wanted to tell her how lucky I was that she was my mom. I wanted to tell her what a great example of strength and compassion she was for us growing up. I wanted to tell her that she was the most amazing woman on the planet and thank her for giving me my life. I wanted to tell her that my failures and mistakes were on me, and that no one could have done a better job being a mother to a son than she'd been to me.

"Nick?" said my sister. "Talk now." She held the phone to my mom's ear.

"Mom," I said, struggling with all my might not to let my voice break. "I love you very, very much."

They were my final words to her. I hope they were enough.

CHAPTER TWENTY

Pandemic 2ⁿᵈ Quarter

I knew, even before dialing my mom's number, somehow I knew. My sister answered. Mom had passed away in the night. My brother Josh had been there on one side of her bed, my sister Jenny on the other, each holding one of her hands as her soul left her body. Jenny told me about how our mother's eyes had lit up with happiness at the sound of my voice the evening before. I still felt like an utter failure as a son. I should have been there by her side, as they were. I should have said more that final time on the phone.

Can you imagine if I'd not made that call? I've said how prison can be a place of horrific cruelty but can also sometimes be a place of unexpected compassion. Ms. Sumpter, our phone coordinator, had not been required to process my mom's cell as an emergency. She could just as easily have made me wait until September 15, when phone lists were normally processed. This would have been bad, since my mom passed away on September 12.

I've heard many prisoners speak ill of Ms. Sumpter. She's not well-liked by the general population; they've called her every bad name for a female in the book, pretty much. You'll never hear me say a harsh word against Ms. Sumpter, though. Ever. Had she not done what she'd done, which, make no mistake, she hadn't had to do, I'd never have had the opportunity for those precious last moments with my mom. It was a gift I could never possibly repay, never come close to repaying.

The main thing I remember about talking to my sister that morning was the weight of the profoundly devastating news I was receiving contrasted with the base and trivial conversations going on around me. The phones were stuck to the wall a mere three feet away from one another with no side walls for privacy, each man could hear every other person's conversation. Men walked up and down the halls yelling, cursing, and laughing, no regard for the men on the phone. I hung up and walked back to my room, struggling to maintain my composure, then got into my bunk and covered up. I cried for I don't know how long. Seemed like hours. Every time I thought I was done another wave would hit.

Prisoners love their mothers. Seems an incredibly simplistic and obvious thing to say, I know; who doesn't love their mother? Yet I believe there may be a deeper connection with prisoners. Everyone is unique, certainly, but a common thread that runs through many prisoners, particularly ones serving long sentences, is the diminution of contact with family and friends over the years. There may be many in your corner at the start of your sentence, but those numbers drop with each passing calendar. For those lucky enough to still have their mothers in their lives, the O.G. (Original Girl) is the one who never fades, come what may. Our mothers do this time with us. Everyone's life is different, but aside from the rare exceptions this is a universal truth.

My mom was there for me through all kinds of lunacy. My military career was less than stellar. I can be honest about it. I received a General Discharge for drug abuse; Turkish hashish over in what was then called West Germany. Still, mom was there. When I got home from the Army she got me an opportunity through her connections at work to enter an apprenticeship program in the heavy crane operator's union. I would be building skyscrapers, dams, and bridges all over the country and around the world. I blew that off so I could move to Chicago to become a famous musician, starting a band with the drummer I'd met in the Army.

Amazingly, my mom was supportive. When I was locked up for first degree murder she hung in tough when everyone else, including my own brothers and sisters, had written me off. I'm sure it's much the same story for many other prisoners. It's messed up that I brought my mom so much pain and disappointment in life because all I ever really wanted to do was make her happy. All I can do now is live the remainder of my life in a way that will make her proud.

The days and weeks following her passing were a blur. I didn't care about much of anything. I told Walt, of course. I told our fearless leader, Ms. Briney, who had been periodically checking in on the Level Up guys that'd been moved to Housing Unit 5. She relayed the news back to Hustle and the others. They made a really beautiful card and sent it to me through the prison smuggler network, the card had an intricate cross with my mother's name, Cathy, inscribed inside it. I still have it. I don't know how the hell they found out her name, I'd never told it to anyone.

I was grieving, but life went on, as it does. Walt received some uplifting news one day around this time. Our mutual friend, Renaldo Hudson (the man who'd trained me to be a peer educator), had been granted clemency. He was out!

Renaldo Hudson's story is amazing, he's a man who literally transformed his life from one extreme to another. He served 30 years in the IDOC, starting his sentence out on death row. His sentence was commuted to life in prison without the possibility of parole in 2002 by then Governor George Ryan when he signed a blanket commutation for all Illinois death row inmates.

Mr. Hudson was that dude back in the day. His institutional disciplinary history paints a grim picture of a young man with some dire antisocial issues; staff assaults, fire bombings, and God only knows what else. The death row guards had to assemble a specialized cell extraction squad just to deal with him. He would often speak of his illiteracy when he first came to prison.

"If the warden had told me that they would let me go if I could spell the word 'A,' I wouldn't have been able to do it," he'd say to a group of newly arrived prisoners in Danville during intake orientation.

His transformation began with turning his life over to God and continued with education. He first earned his GED then completed various vocational and college courses. He earned his Associate's Degree. He became involved in Education Justice Project (EJP). He earned his Associate's in theology at the seminary school in Danville and was a peer educator. He was instrumental in developing and implementing the Building Block Program at Danville, the program upon which Level Up is based. He was chapel clerk for Chaplain Easton.

Today Renaldo works tirelessly for the Illinois Prison Project where he is either preparing for, going to, or coming from a meeting with someone in authority with whom he advocates on prisoners' behalf. Few were more deserving of clemency than Renaldo Hudson.

Except me!

Mr. Hudson's success gave me great hope because if they'd granted his clemency, then they absolutely HAD to grant mine! I had all kinds of letters of support and multiple IDOC staff as character references. I was a military veteran, had a minor IDOC disciplinary history and no prior criminal history, and 22 years in. I was going home! No way around it.

Yeah, right.

Chapter Twenty-One

Pandemic 2nd Quarter

Time dragged on. It was around then, in later October, that we heard about COVID claiming its first prisoner in Jacksonville. An older gentleman named Bob who'd worked in the inmate commissary had passed away due to complications from the virus. I hope everyone who attended C/O Patty's retirement party had a good time, at least. They were paying the cover charge in human life.

I didn't know Bob, not really, but I'd seen him around. He'd actually been one of my roommates in COVID House, one of the guys on the CPAP machines. I really hate to hear about anyone passing away in prison. I don't wish that on anyone.

Bob hadn't been the old moaning guy, the one I'd told, "Go ahead and die, but whatever you do, shut...the fuck...up!" Thank God for that, I'd've felt horrible. No, the old moaning guy had been a man that everyone called "Old Man Martin." Old Man Martin is still alive and well as of this writing, just as whiny and annoying as he ever was.

I buried myself in my Blackstone studies. I was grinding through those books like nobody's business. I was determined to do well in honor of my mother's memory, who'd paid my tuition for that course. There wasn't much else going on. We still weren't being allowed to go anywhere or do anything. Food, if you want to call it that, was still being brought to the housing units. Officers were still avoiding wings. Unless we were killing each other or burning the place down, we had a free pass to do whatever.

Just when we thought they might be getting ready to loosen the restrictions, an inmate commissary supervisor, Ms. B, tested positive for the virus. They had been spot testing staff at that time. They immediately quarantined all the inmate commissary workers in a total overreaction. If only they'd acted that way back in the beginning when it would have made a difference. They put the workers in the tents, but let's face it, what they were doing was like the fire department showing up to a fire after the building had already burned down, then started spraying the smoldering ashes with water.

"Hey, uhh…that would've been great awhile ago, fellas, but it's a little late now. There's nothing left to save."

Same principle with them quarantining the workers. Everyone in the entire facility, save none, had already contracted the virus. Who were they trying to protect? As an afterthought, they sent the inmate clothing and property workers to the tents, also, since they all worked in the same building. They would all be in the tents for at least 14 days.

Ironically, Ms. B was back at work again the next day. Nah, I'm sure it was fine. They knew best. Commissary was being brought to the housing units, so Ms. B was only interacting with a small number of EVERY SINGLE PRISONER INSIDE THE FACILITY. No, we're good, though. Sure.

With all the commissary workers hemmed up in the quarantine tents, they called on none other than my boys Walt and Nelly to volunteer as commissary workers. Once they got over there, the commissary supervisor, Mr. Brownfield…Brumfeld…Bloomfield? Something, whatever. He asked Nelly if he knew anyone else who he'd recommend as a volunteer.

"Hell no, I don't mess with none of these goofies like that," Nelly replied.

"What about Nick?" asked Walt.

"Oh, yeah, I'd vouch for Nick," said Nelly. "He'd be the only one, though."

"Who?" asked Brinefold.

"Chittick," said Walt.

"Chittick...Chittick...I know that name," said Ms. B. "Didn't he die out on the yard a couple months back?"

"No, he's fine," said Nelly and Walt.

"Isn't he crippled or something? Can he even do this job?" asked Mr. Blunnford.

"Well...only one way to find out," Walt replied.

When they came back in from work that day, Walt asked me, "Do you think you could handle working commissary?"

"I think so," I replied. "If I had to. Why?"

"You're coming to work with us tomorrow."

Working at the inmate commissary was enlightening. I'd been wondering what the deal was with Jacksonville's inmate commissary ever since I'd first gotten there. At every other prison's commissary that I'd experienced, they might be out of a particular item. Maybe even two or three items every now and then, but usually they had everything in stock. Jacksonville's commissary was always out of stuff, they've still, as of this writing, never once had everything in stock any time I've ever shopped over there. They're always out of things, usually many things. One time they were out of every single item on my list. Literally every item. We were down to near half capacity at a little over 500 inmates and they were *still* always out of stuff. Now that I was going to be working over there I was going to get to the bottom of things and get shit in order over there.

It didn't take long to figure out what the problem was. Jacksonville commissary was always out of items because the people in charge of the commissary weren't commissary supervisors. Ms. B and Mr. Brungfailed were correctional officers. They had the job title of commissary supervisor, they wore civilian clothing to work, but they had started out as C/Os and still were at heart.

They didn't believe prisoners should even be allowed to purchase the things sold on commissary. That's why they were always out of everything. They didn't care. Ms. B actually said, "If it were up to me, you'd only be allowed to buy cosmetics and write outs," shortly after I started working there. For you unincarcerated people, a write out is a pre-stamped envelope that we use to send letters to our families and loved ones. Ms. B and Mr. Bronnfelled liked putting the cables on one another, geeking each other up to mistreat the prisoners in some petty way. They made sport of it. Being around them was unbearable. My tongue is now permanently lined with deep scars because of how many times I had to bite it working over there.

"There isn't an inmate benefit fund generated by the commissary. It's called the commissary fund," said Mr. Brainfeeled one day.

"Yeah?" I replied. "Then where's the inmate benefit fund come from?" I asked. I already knew the answer; he was talking out of his ass. He didn't like the fact that it was called the inmate benefit fund and felt it should be called the commissary fund.

"I don't know if inmate benefit fund is even a thing anymore," he said.

Man, I wanted to go in on him. He could get away with telling some newbie something like that, but I'd been doing time in the IDOC since he was in middle school. I opened my mouth to speak when I saw Walt watching me from across the way. He was giving me this look that said, "Get out of there." I knew that look. It was the same one he'd give from behind the drumkit when I'd miss a note during a song. I knew full well that the IBF consisted of 25 percent of inmate commissary sales, and I knew that there was no such thing as a commissary fund. I bit my tongue, though.

My first day there a worker named Tex asked Ms. B, "Someone said you tested positive for coronavirus the day before yesterday."

"I did," she replied. "that's why you guys are working over here, our other workers had to quarantine for 14 days."

"But…aren't you supposed to be on quarantine too?" Tex asked.

"I did. I was out for 14 days."

"But…I thought you just tested positive the day before yesterday."

"Yes," she said, aggression and an unmistakable threat now in her tone. "I tested positive the day before yesterday, then I was out for 14 days, and now I'm back at work to earn money. Do you have a problem with that or something?"

She wasn't supposed to be back at work yet. The way she blatantly flaunted the truth was like a bully in the schoolyard holding your lunchbox over your head as they chanted, "I don't have your lunch box! I don't have your lunch box!" I hated working in commissary not because it was hard work (although it was), but because of having to be around those two idiots.

The commissary supervisor who absolutely took the cake, though, was a man named Ortega. If you saw this guy on the street you'd think he was definitely a homeless person. Long, ratty, uncombed hair, a long and scraggly beard paired to a face that looked as though it had seen decades of harsh, outdoor living. The rumor was that Ortega never spent a dime on clothing because his entire wardrobe consisted of clothes pilfered from the inmate donation closet.

There is a large room designated the inmate donation closet. It consisted of all brands of shoes, boots, jeans, t-shirts, button-ups, jackets, etc. This clothing was intended for inmates who were going home with nothing to wear. Jacksonville would kick them out the door with a decent outfit or two. There was a large window on the door to the room so you could look in and see what they had. Some pretty nice stuff in there, really. You'd be surprised.

Anyway, people said that was where Ortega got all his clothes. You know how people like to talk. I don't know if it's true that he got all of his clothes from the inmate donation closet, but one thing I do know is that one day there was a nice Carhartt jacket hanging in the closet, a black one. The next day it was gone, and Ortega was wearing a nice, black Carhartt jacket. Coincidence? Me thinks not.

Another thing *they* (*they* talk a lot) say is that Ortega's garage at home looks like a Keefe warehouse. Keefe is one of IDOC's main vendors for the inmate commissary. Staff commissary too, for that matter. Now, I don't know if that's true or not, either, but one thing I do know is what happened one day when Walt was helping him stock inventory in the warehouse.

Many times when a truck comes in there will be a box of sample products not included in the shipping order. There was one such box on the day Walt was helping Ortega stock the incoming inventory.

"Looks like we got a box of samples here, Ortega," said Walt.

Ortega immediately dropped what he was doing, setting his clipboard down and making a beeline for the box in question. He looked inside, his eyes widening. There were various bags of chips, boxes of cakes, packs of cookies, and other goodies.

"Oh, I gotta get this to the car," said Ortega quietly, under his breath.

"What?" said Walt.

"Huh?"

"What'd you say just now?" Walt asked, pressing.

"I didn't say anything," Ortega insisted. "Not out loud."

Walt just laughed. He'd heard Ortega clearly. Ortega was a little slow, maybe, and bit OCD, perhaps some mild form of autism, but he wasn't a bad guy. He was totally incompetent at his job, yeah, but he didn't have the disdain and venom in his heart for prisoners that Ms. B and Mr. Bernfailed did. He was just a simple-minded guy who really, really liked to steal. Couldn't hold that against him. Many of my fellow prisoners, and Ortega's fellow staff members, suffered from the same inclination. Luckily for Ortega and his coworkers, they'd chosen an occupation where they could do so with complete impunity.

BREAKING NEWS: Prison Employees Steal

OTHER BREAKING NEWS: Ice is Cold

The one bright spot about working at the inmate commissary was the correctional officer who worked security there; Ms. Cheeks. She was a real sweetheart. Well, at least she was if she liked you. If she didn't like you, watch out. How to get her to like you? Don't be an idiot. She had purchased a can of real coffee (not instant) for us to brew in the commissary coffee maker, paying for it out of her own pocket. A small perk for volunteering. We weren't getting paid, after all. Ms. B and Mr. Barnfurled hated that, boy, but they couldn't do anything about it because Ms. Cheeks was security and had the final say.

Ms. B and Mr. Brungfold weren't the only reason working there was a pain. There were a couple of our inmate coworkers who knew how to tap dance on your last nerve. One man in particular comes to mind. Brian Abel. Not our Unstable Abel, but a different Brian Abel. He did so much stupid shh…stuff that it would be impossible to describe it all in these pages. He's his own book. His biography would be called, "In the Way: The Brian Abel Story."

I'll give you an example of a possible Brian Abel experience. Here's how commissary worked; a prisoner would fill out a commissary list, then submit it. We were bringing commissary to the housing units, we could grab a list off the stack and place the items on that list into a plastic container, then bring it to one of the two checkout windows.

Now imagine you're filling your guy's list out.

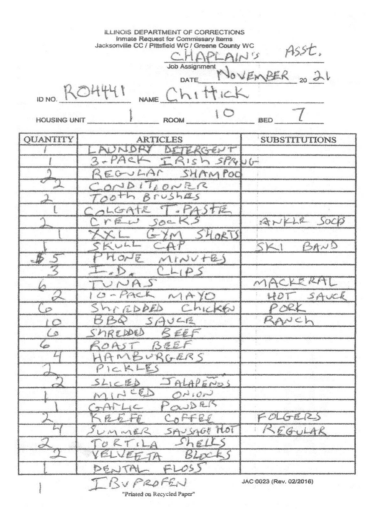

Figure 11: Commissary Form

He orders six tunas. So, you grab six tunas off the shelf, then place them in your container. Every worker had a spot for their particular container. After you drop the six tunas in your container, here comes Brian Abel and takes two of them out.

"Hey! What are you doing?"

"I need two tunas for this list."

"Fine, so go to the aisle where the tunas are and get your own, don't take them out of my guy's container."

"But you had six. I only need two."

"My guy ordered six, not four! Don't take shit from my box!"

"But I needed them. They were right there. The tunas are all the way over there."

'DON'T TAKE SHIT OUT OF MY CONTAINER!"

End scene. This has been a simulation of an authentic Brian Abel experience. This is what we were dealing with.

One time, ol' Brian Abel got under Nelly's skin. Being responsible global citizens, Jacksonville recycles. The inmate commissary generated vast amounts of cardboard, as I'm sure you can imagine. We would break boxes down and place them in these huge nylon or canvas bags. It would take two people to drag these bags outside and place them in line for pick up.

Brian Abel had gotten into the habit of asking Nelly to help him with this task in front of Ms. B and Mr. Bernflood. Nelly couldn't very well tell him to go fu…fornicate with himself, not in front of our bosses. One day Brian Abel did it again, right in front of our bosses. Again.

"Hey, Nelly, how about you give me a hand with this cardboard?"

Nelly smiled his best Sambo-Bojangles smile and said, "Hey! Sure, buddy, come on, I got you!"

As soon as they stepped through the doors and were out of our supervisors' earshot, though, Nelly's smile vanished. He turned.

"Check this out, mutha fucka, stop asking me to do this shit. I ain't over here to work. You want somebody to work, ask one of these Mexicans, that's what they're here for. But from now on, miss me with this bullshit."

Then Nelly pushed Brian Abel into the bathroom and brutally beat and raped him.

No, just kidding. I made up that last part. Nelly isn't that type of person, he's a good brother with a good heart. He's actually a good worker too, despite his comment to Brian Abel that he wasn't, "...over here to work." He'd have helped any of us with that cardboard, and in fact, did so all the time, he just didn't want to do it for Brian Abel. That guy got on all of our nerves.

A man named Pat was Ms. B and Mr. Burnfulled's boss, he was the clothing supervisor. Pat would allow the inmate workers to buy sodas and snacks from the inmate commissary at lunch time, as has traditionally been the case at every other prison in the IDOC for as long as I've been in the IDOC. Inmate workers were allowed to buy snacks. That's always been a given.

If Pat wasn't at work that day, though, Ms. B and Mr. Bronefulled wouldn't allow it.

"You guys don't need to be over here drinking sodas and eating snacks," he said one day as he was nibbling on free sample chips and sipping on a Diet Pepsi. He and Ms. B believed they were better than prisoners and blatantly broadcasted this belief on a daily basis through their words and actions. And Ms. B had the audacity to regularly wear a "Jesus Saves" t-shirt to work.

"This people honors Me with their lips, but their heart is far from me..." Mark 7:6.

In her defense, that scripture could also be used against me by the casual observer. Also, judge not lest ye be judged.

Our weekly spending limit was increased to $100 per week, up from $30. Ms. B and Mr. Brownflailed hated that. Then, when a federal judge ruled that the language and intent of Trump's stimulus package was that every prisoner receive a stimulus check, hoo-boy. You'd have thought the money was coming out of their personal bank accounts. Free Trump Fun Bucks for all the killers, drug dealers, rapists, and pedophiles. Yee haw! Thanks, Donny.

About the time we found out that we were all going to receive stimulus checks we learned that COVID had claimed its second victim in Jacksonville. This time it was our friend, Big Swole. The story was that they'd waited too long before taking him to an outside hospital. I don't know if that's true, but I do know that both Bob and Swole had passed away shortly after arriving at the outside hospital, according to reports.

This would seem to support the hypothesis that they'd waited too long.

Big Swole had survived decades of danger in some of the IDOC's worst prisons, he'd even been shot by a guard in Stateville, and in the end he was taken out by a retirement party. Officer Patty and her guests were racking up a body count, but they weren't done yet. More deaths would come.

PRISON WAR STORIES

Walt, Nelly, and myself weren't the only ones going through difficult times. Back in Housing Unit 1, the Level Up Program had been put through the wringer. In our absence they'd moved a bunch of nonparticipants onto the wing.

Here's the thing about trying to run any kind of program in a prison setting; you can't have half of the guys who are on board, respecting the rules about cleanliness and respect, while the other half are saying, "Man, fuck this deck! I'm throwing my trash on the floor, I'm pissing on the toilet seats, I'm leaving my hair in the sink, and I'm throwing used bars of soap on the floor in the shower. I didn't sign up for this shit, when they're trying to do these punk-ass group sessions I'm going to be in the dayroom making as much noise as possible." It doesn't work that way. It's a recipe for disaster.

This is what Hustle, Chavez, B, and the rest of the mentors and participants had been dealing with. Even more, Chavez had been dealing with family trouble; divorce. His wife had decided to leave him in the midst of the pandemic, seizing control of his bank accounts, home, vehicles, and was playing defense on him speaking with his children. This, coupled with the fact that officers had been seizing his weight bags and ordering him not to workout in the dayroom, became the backdrop for what became known as the "Chavez Juice Incident."

The situation was already somewhat of a pressure cooker. They woke everyone up in the middle of the night at 3:30 am to take their temperatures. It was all just for show, everyone had already contracted the virus.

Divorce. Restricted from working out. Locked indoors for weeks upon weeks. Nonparticipants disrespecting the program he'd worked so hard to put together. Chavez waited in line for breakfast (which was served right after temperature checks) with all of these elements swirling about in his groggy mind.

He reached the end of the serving line. The officer handed the guy right in front of Chavez the last tray. Chavez stepped up. The officer had nothing to give him.

"Do you want a tray?" the C/O demanded, annoyed and slightly aggressive, as though Chavez were bothering him. Calling the chow hall for extra trays would be a major hassle.

"Do I want a tray?" Chavez said quietly, almost as if to himself. "Do I want a tray?" he repeated, louder this time. "You wake me up in the middle of the night for this phony-ass shit, and then you ask me do I want a MOTHER FUCKING TRAY!"

By that time Chavez was screaming. A switch had been flipped somewhere in his brain. Changing tactics, the officer tried to appease Chavez.

"Here, you can have an extra juice," he said, handing Chavez a juice. Normally you were only allowed one.

Chavez stepped back and looked at the two juices in his hand as though they were artifacts from a lost alien culture.

"Juice?" he said. "JUICE! I'LL THROW THESE PUNK-ASS JUICES AGAINST THE WALL RIGHT NOW, FUCK THESE JUICES. YOU MOTHER FUCKERS ARE GONNA GET ENOUGH OF PLAYING GAMES WITH ME, I'LL STOMP ONE OF YOU BITCHES THE FUCK OUT!"

The officer hurried off the deck, terrified. He wrote Chavez an IDR for the incident. The officer who presided over the hearing took pity, he understood the bogus circumstances we were living under.

The punishment?

Two weeks of unit restriction at a time when we were already on total lockdown. In this context, Chavez walked away with a win.

CHAPTER TWENTY-TWO

Pandemic 2nd Quarter

We tried to bring outside attention to what was going on inside Jacksonville, but no one cared. The average reaction of the general public to the news that men and women in prison are being mistreated is, "Oh, they're mistreating the criminals in prison? Well, good, that's what they *should* be doing."

Walt's niece called a local television journalist, a kind of "Local Five on Your Side" type of deal. She told him how we weren't being provided the proper cleaning supplies or hand sanitizer. The only hand sanitizer we were getting was going into and then coming out of the chow hall, and we weren't going to the chow hall.

"Your uncle is lying to you," the journalist told Walt's niece. "The prisoners in the IDOC are being provided with all the necessary hygiene items they need. I talked to an IDOC spokesperson in Springfield, and they told me so theirself."

Walt's niece was a Chicago-raised young lady. Her suggestion on how to address the issue was to, "...wait for that bitch and beat his ass in the parking lot of his news station."

"No, no," said Walt, ever the voice of reason to people both inside and outside prison. "It ain't that serious."

Coincidentally, about this same time there was a news segment on local media about the IDOC response to the virus. They talked to an IDOC spokesperson.

"We are working closely with the Illinois Department of Public Health to ensure the safety of both IDOC employees and the committed persons (fancy name for prisoner) at all of our facilities."

Then they cut to an interview with an Illinois Department of Public Health spokesperson.

"The IDOC has ignored our advice at every turn. They refuse to do comprehensive testing, they won't allow us access to any of their facilities, and at this point they aren't returning any of our calls."

It might have been amusing if not for the dire consequences of the IDOC's actions.

I wrote at least a dozen letters to various prisoner rights law firms; Uptown People's Law Center, Loevy & Loevy, Christopher Smith Trial Group, Ed Fox & Associates, Craig M. Sandberg, Pinix & Soukup, Gil Sapir, and others. I explained in my letters how COVID had gotten into Jacksonville. Most of them didn't even bother to write back despite the fact that I'd included a self-addressed-stamped envelope with each of my letters to them. The ones that did write back weren't interested in helping us.

Hundreds of us filed grievances about the COVID retirement party and how the virus entered the facility. We all received variations of the same response.

"Prisoners need not concern themselves with what staff does on their off-duty hours, there is no proof of who attended this alleged party, and if there were proof, there was still no proof that such persons contracted the virus or, if they did contract the virus, there was no proof they brought it into the facility, it's a worldwide pandemic, deal with it." It was frustrating, but not surprising.

In October, word went out to the Level Up people who had been displaced by the quarantine charade that Jacksonville had been perpetrating could now return to Housing Unit 1, back to the program.

We were each asked if we wanted to return. Almost everyone said yes. Nelly was hesitant at first just because moving was such a hassle. He tried to say no, but Ms. Briney wasn't trying to hear it. Even Walt wasn't crazy about the idea of leaving Housing Unit 5 because he had such a sweet phone situation there. He would be returning to a place where far more people used the phones, which meant that his daily allotted minutes speaking with Shamekia would be cut down. He bit the bullet, though.

The day that he and I returned to Housing Unit 1 with the other participants we received a hero's welcome, as though we were liberating them from an enemy occupation. In a way, I suppose we were. As we were moving in, the nonparticipants who had been such a disruptive presence were moving out, the Level Up guys formed a spectator line as they filed out of the building in defeat. Level Uppers were clapping, shouting, and carrying on.

"Yeah! That's right! Get your nasty, trifling, dumbass, ho-ass, bitch-ass selves up off our deck, punk mother fuckers! SHA NA NA NA, SHA NA NA NA, HEY, HEY, HEY, SUCK OUR DICKS!"

Okay, maybe it didn't happen quite that way. That's how I remember it, though. We moved right back into our same bunks. I was hit with a deluge of legal work, right in the door.

"Hey, Nick, glad you're back, bro. I was real sorry to hear about your mom. Anyway, I got this court deadline and I really need a motion for a…"

Chavez, Hustle, and the other mentors told us how they had powered through all sorts of obstacles and challenges to keep the program going. The day they moved all the nonparticipants onto the wing Officer Marshall had taken it upon himself to cancel the program. He made the announcement as the riffraff were moving in.

"Hey, guys, this program is done. I want these chairs and all these books and boxes of papers out of here. Bring them out here, we'll store them in the laundry room for now. Level Up is done. It's over."

Chavez came into the room as inmates were stacking chairs. Marshall was standing at the door with his arms crossed.

"What the hell are you guys doing?" asked Chavez.

"The C/O said get these chairs and books out of here, the program is over."

"Man, fuck Fat Boy," Chavez replied, right in front of Marshall. "He ain't in charge of nothing. Put those chairs down and leave those books and boxes alone."

This infuriated Marshall. Chavez hadn't simply challenged his authority, he'd completely derided it in front of several other inmates. Plus, he'd fired a shot about Marshall's weight.

"Hey! I said get that stuff out of here, this program is over!"

Faced with two conflicting orders, one from Chavez and another from a C/O, the prisoners simply abandoned their task and walked away, preferring not to get involved in the conflict.

"Hey!" said Marshall to the prisoners. "Hey, I'm telling you what's going to happen! I'm not asking!"

"Our program coordinator didn't tell us anything," said Chavez. "If you want these chairs and books off the deck, get a lieutenant over here and have him tell us. This program isn't over until Ms. Briney says it is."

Marshall was fuming. He'd tried, can't blame a guy for trying. Marshall was one of a significant number of staff who believed that Level Up was simply, "...inmates running inmates." As much as it angered him, he couldn't pursue it further because he knew he was bogus, that he'd had no official authorization to dismantle the program.

Marshall retaliated against Chavez by having another officer write him an IDR for Failure to Wear a Mask. Side note, this is how far circle we'd come in the IDOC. In frigid, subzero-degree weather if you tried to cover your face with a ski band or scarf, you'd get an IDR for Attempting to Conceal Identity. Now we were getting IDRs for Failure to Wear a Mask. Totes cray-cray, and not in a good way.

In a karmic twist, when they delivered this new and latest IDR to Chavez, they accidentally gave him the entire document instead of just his yellow copy off the back. Chavez, never one to miss an opportunity when it came knocking, promptly shredded the document and flushed it. What IDR? Marshall was never the wiser.

It seemed that Chavez was having good luck with IDRs, at least, if in no other area of his life at that time.

Chapter Twenty-Three

Pandemic 3rd Quarter

When we'd come back to the program, they were already in the middle of another 10-week cycle, week five. I joined Buddha as his co-facilitator/co-mentor. The Level Up participants decided to host a welcome home party for those of us who'd returned to the fold.

Food was prepared in abundance; pizzas, quesadillas, burritos, burgers, nachos, and more. JD, the ultra-conservative, Trump-worshipping, diehard Republican who had been my bunk neighbor in Room 4 back before the pandemic, prepared a large batch of hooch that'd been fermenting for weeks.

There'd been a large donation of strawberries made to the institution. Dietary Superintendent White, true to form, had been giving these strawberries to the staff only. But there were far more strawberries on hand than only the staff could consume. Fortunately, there were a few industrious prisoners who were in possession of the necessary testicular fortitude to covertly procure a very large amount of these strawberries and make certain that they were generously distributed to the proper recipients; us.

Although an undertaking such as this undoubtedly required the participation and cooperation of many different individuals, I'm certain that Hustle was involved at one or more key points in the chain of custody. It's just who he was.

This large amount of strawberries, overly ripe and on the verge of fermentation, combined with several crates of fruit juice and a couple pounds of sugar, made for some of the best prison wine, if not the best, I'd ever tasted, both in terms of flavor and alcohol content. Sugar is what converted to alcohol during the fermentation process. JD knocked it out of the park, truly. Credit where credit is due.

I hadn't intended to get drunk. Let me say that first. I had set up my desk in my bunk and was catching up on legal work. "Setting up my desk" was when I rolled my mattress up and out of the way, then set my property box on the metal slab of the bunk. Then I'd set my typewriter on my property box, the surface of which is about 4' by 2'. It serves as a poor man's desk. It's what I'm doing right now as I type these words. Hang my book light on the top bunk, shining down onto my work area, and I'm ready for business.

It's precisely what I was doing on the night of the party when JD came into the room and asked Walt and I if we'd like a cup of wine.

"It came out really good," he said.

I hadn't partaken of the hooch in quite a long time. It'd been years. As far as substance abuse issues go, I know I've conquered my drug problems. I've never used cocaine in prison over the years despite many opportunities to do so. The thought of doing cocaine makes me feel ill. As far as marijuana…

We don't have to talk about that right now.

JD had asked a question, though. Do I want a cup of wine? Hmm. You know what? Why not? Walt and I both said yes to JD's gracious offer. One wasn't going to kill us. Famous last words.

JD set a cup down on my desk and I stopped typing to take a sip.

"Damn…this is pretty good, actually," I said.

Usually, drinking hooch meant enduring a highly unpleasant flavor just to get the alcoholic effects. JD's vintage was a rare mix of excellent taste and moonshine kick. It wasn't Ernest & Julio Gallo, but it as a damn sight better than Mad Dog 20/20. Before Walt had a chance to try his he was called away to the card table.

"Here, Nick, drink mine," said Walt, placing his cup on my desk. "I gotta keep a clear head for this card table."

"Okay, but I had only planned on drinking one," I said.

"Well, now you can drink two."

If only.

I took sips on the first one, nursing it, really enjoying it. I took drinks on the second one, maybe a gulp or two, and it was gone more quickly. My work started to suffer. Typos emerged at an alarming rate. I was legally impaired, as law enforcement professionals liked to say. The person I was doing the legal work for, Red, came in to consult with me. He saw the two empty cups on my desk.

"Hey, Tricky Nicky, how's it coming with the…oh, are you drinking, man?" asked Red.

"Nah, not really. I just had a couple."

"Hey, man, I'm just saying. I got like three pitchers of this stuff. I'd have offered you some, but I've never seen you drinking when we made batches before."

"I usually don't. I figured, what the hell, you know?"

"So, do you want another?"

"Sure. If it was good enough for Jesus, it's good enough for me. Your work is going to have to wait until tomorrow, though."

"Oh, that's cool, man, fuck it. It's a party!"

I put my typewriter away and broke my desk down. Things get a bit hazy after that. A few of us set up shop in the back of Room 10. Hustle, JD, Red, Serb, D-Block, myself, and a few others. Chavez was floating around here and there. Walt let me hook up my tablet to his black Panasonic radio so we could rock some tunes. We ate too much. When my cup got low one time, Serb (his nickname was Serb, which was short for Serbia, but he was actually Croatian) refilled it while I wasn't looking. After that they turned it into the game of "Keep Nick's Cup Full." Allegedly, I told Walt, "I love you, man," in a drunken slur at some point. At another point in the evening I apparently made a speech. I got absolutely plastered, along with half the deck. I don't know how I stayed upright for temperature checks that night.

We'd have never gotten away with such debauchery prior to the pandemic, nor would we today. Then, however, in the midst of the COVID restrictions gripping not just the IDOC, but the entire nation and the world, the guards left us to fend for ourselves.

You may be saying to yourself, "See? They really are just animals. They're supposed to be in a program to better themselves and they're brewing hooch and getting drunk." To you I would say, lighten up, Nancy Grace.

I would point out what DIDN'T happen. Number one, no one got hurt and there were no fights. This was remarkable when you consider the different races, cultures, age groups, and life views. There were killers and drug dealers. There were no pedophiles or rapists because people with those cases were prohibited from participation in Level Up. Let them have the GEO Program.

Level Up was a program we all felt very strongly about. It was ours. Issues were handled internally without intervention from staff, and the vibe on the night of the party was a very positive one. It was almost like a homecoming, strange as that is to say about a prison setting.

Secondly, no one in AA who was actively in recovery was allowed to drink. Not even JD, who had brewed the batch, had partaken. Recovery was respected.

We were a group of human beings living through extraordinary circumstances, and we needed to blow off a little steam. It wasn't something we did every day, and it was actually healthy. Probably. At the very least it wasn't harmful. The worst consequences of that night were the hangovers the next day. People in the free world certainly weren't avoiding the liquor stores during the pandemic.

Why was that alright for them and not for us?

CHAPTER TWENTY-FOUR

Pandemic 3ʳᵈ Quarter

I was once again living a purpose-driven life. I jumped in to facilitating groups full force. Level Up was back in action 100 percent. I was reenergized. I amended and refiled my lawsuit against Wexford. This time my case was assigned before the Honorable Joe Billy McDade. Thanks to a modest inheritance from my mother, plus the stimulus payments I had coming from Donald J. Trump, I was now able to pay for the cost of litigation.

Thank the Lord for my Blackstone studies because the prison law library had been closed since the start of the pandemic. The so-called law librarian, who'd taken over the assignment from a man named Boyd (who did a great job), was a man named George Strode. He was a straight-up punk bitch who wasn't even performing notary services. He sent these arrogant, pissant responses to prisoner's requests, including several of mine, talking about how he wasn't going to jeopardize his health over our legal papers, the law library was closed indefinitely, and yadda yadda whatever. His health. His punk-ass was probably one of the ones who brought the virus into the facility in the first place with his trifling disease ridden…you know what? Wuu-saa. Tranquility now. Sorry. I get a little heated when discussing Mr. Strode. I strongly dislike that bitch. Sorry. I strongly dislike that fellow.

Shortly after we reconstructed and reunited the program to full potential our fearless leader, Ms. Briney, came over and called a mentor meeting. She had obtained permission from the powers-that-be to hold the meeting outside. She came in wearing full PPE.

"Would you like to go outside?" she asked. "Get a little fresh air?"

"Hell, yeah!" we replied. Aside from walking to and from our job assignments, or moving from one housing unit to another, none of us had spent any amount of time outside since we'd gone back on total lockdown quarantine.

We went out in front of the housing unit, onto the patio. Or at least it was what they called a patio. It was four stone tables plopped down onto a patch of muddy weeds and grass. Still, it was outside. It may as well have been the White House rose garden on that nice, bright, cloudless afternoon, unseasonably warm.

We discussed the future of the program going forward. She assured us that they would never again move nonparticipants onto the wing. We had a new program warden (the institution's number two in charge), Warden "Auggie" they called him. I believe his real name is Augustus or something like that. He actually came from Graham, he'd been part of their Healthcare Unit Administration as a psych doctor. Word through inmate Twitter was that Springfield had finally had enough of Graham's substandard healthcare and had disbanded and reassigned their entire HCU administration, refilling those vacated positions with competent people. I don't know if that's true, but it's certainly plausible.

Anyway, the new warden was on board with the program. Springfield was on board with the program, and things were looking up. Man, that sun was bright. Ms. Briney said something about a guy named Van Winkle.

"Who?" I asked.

"Van Winkle," she replied. "The head of Clinical Services? No? Really, Mr. Chittick? He's the guy in charge of this program."

"He is? Because I've never met him. I've never even seen him, I don't think."

"You didn't miss anything," said Hustle. "He's a straight lame."

"Okay, guys, stop," scolded Ms. Briney. "Let's stay focused and get back on track."

"Can we finish this up inside?" asked someone. "It's too bright out here."

There was a chorus of agreement.

"Yeah, let's go in. This sun is giving me a headache," said someone else.

Coming outside had seemed like a good idea, but the reality of it didn't quite match up. It was as though we were underground cave dwellers who'd emerged from our subterranean habitat unprepared for the giant ball of sky-fire blasting its deadly rays down upon us pale, sickly creatures as we cowered from the light. "Arrgg, nooo! Hiss! It burns, it burns!"

We went back inside. Ms. Briney was withdrawn and distant for the remainder of the meeting. I thought we'd somehow made her angry, but I later found out that she'd been fighting back tears. As soon as the meeting was over, she made a beeline straight for the Administration Building, all set to raise hell.

"Why aren't we letting these guys go outside?" she demanded. "You've had them locked inside for months! Why? It's not right!"

She was met with amused indifference.

"Oh, Ms. Briney, you're so silly. It's a pandemic, we can do whatever we want to these guys. Who cares if they go outside? They're just a bunch of criminals."

That word "criminal" is powerful. It can be applied to justify all manner of cruelty and mistreatment. As Fire Marshall Bill used to say (Google it), "Let me show you something!"

Take the following statement:

"American citizens have had far too many rights for far too long. We need to strip Americans of these rights so it will be easier to put them in prison and keep them there longer."

How do you feel about that statement? Now watch.

"Criminals have had far too many rights for far too long. We need to strip criminals of these rights so it will be easier to put them in prison and keep them there longer."

See what happens when we add the magic word? When you use that word, the men and women you're speaking of cease to be human, they become *the other. Them. Animals.*

They're not like us.

There's a subtle racism imbedded in that word. A common term used by correctional officers, what do you think a white C/O is really saying when they call one of their coworkers an "inmate lover?" Doesn't take much of a leap in logic to figure it out.

When I hear the pundits debating the existence of systemic racism, it's almost comical. Of course America is inherently racist! It's observable. I saw this as a white man with no guilt whatsoever. I don't have a stake in the debate, but it's just me stating a fact, like grass is green or the sky is blue.

Me being white, my fellow Caucasian correctional staff have let slip the mask of their political correctness many times over the years in my presence. I've overheard an officer telling another one how he loved working in prison because it was, "...one place where you can still treat a nigger like a nigger."

A staff member here in Jacksonville once mentioned to me in a hushed, conspiratorial tone, "at least Trump is a lot better than that nigger, Obama."

I was locked up with a former Springfield police officer in Graham. He was also a veteran, and therefore, was in the veteran house, same as me. I once overheard him say, "The only thing worse than all these niggers in prison is the niggers out there that we haven't put in prison yet."

He was a cop in Springfield for years and years. You think he didn't take that attitude to work every day? You think he was, "one bad apple?" Do you really believe that this mindset wasn't shared by his fellow officers? Be real. We may have come a long way, but the question is, "Does systemic racism exist today?"

Absolutely. In abundance.

I know there are those who will believe that my disclosure of words spoken between whites in private is "bad form." Whenever *they* have floated racist comments like these my way over the years, there is always that quiet moment of realization when I don't cosign what they are saying; "Uh oh! He's one of those!" they think to themselves. Once the mask has slipped, there's no cleaning it up.

Race has always been hyper-magnified in prison. Maybe not as much in Illinois as in other states, but still magnified. In Menard there'd been a white pride organization known as the North Siders. They're found throughout the IDOC's institutions statewide. I got along well with many of them during my years in Menard, and I actually do respect the premise upon which they were formed, to prevent nongang-member whites from being victimized by the various prison organizations comprised of other races.

Based on my free association with those of other races, one of the North Siders came up with a clever nickname for me. He called me Nicker, and the name stuck. That became my name to those guys the rest of my time down there. Good one, I gotta admit.

I must be an inmate lover.

Sorry, I got a little off topic there. I tend to do that, as you've no doubt noticed by now. My whole point, way back when I started (where Ms. Briney was upset about the way we prisoners were being treated) was that it's easy to mistreat others if you believe they are something less than you are. That goes for anyone of any race. And the word *criminal* is designed to do just that, to dehumanize those upon whom the term is conferred.

I don't know if Ms. Briney's advocacy on our behalf had anything to do with what happened next, but shortly after her little outburst they started allowing us to go outside again. Two rooms at a time, yard, a maximum of 40 prisoners, for a half-hour twice a week. Plus patio for about 45 minutes every other day, so about three hours outside per week. There was still no weights or sports equipment, but it was a slight shift back in the direction of normalcy.

One baby step at a time.

CHAPTER TWENTY-FIVE

Pandemic 3ʳᵈ Quarter

Jacksonville continued bleeding prisoners, our numbers were well below 500, closing in on 450. November 6ᵗʰ came and brought with it the much anticipated defeat of Donny Trump, our Brain Dead Cheeto Cheese Puff In-Chief. My boy JD and many of the C/Os were beside themselves with grief. Meanwhile, Democrats and "never Trumper" Republicans danced in the streets with joy when Biden was declared the winner.

Funny how the people who were so adamant about quarantine and social distancing threw those rules out the window when it suited them; there was no social distancing and damn little mask wearing during the summer Black Lives Matter protests, nor during the Sleep Joe celebrations. Just an observation.

November brought other events. There was talk of a vaccine coming out soon. I finally graduated from Blackstone Career Institute. After 31 textbooks, 31 exams, and six written assignments I received my certification as a paralegal. I opened the envelope and looked at my diploma. I'd graduated with distinction thanks to a 97.4 GPA. I looked at my grade transcripts:

Introduction to Law 100%
Contracts Part I 100%
Contracts Part II 100%
Contracts Part III 100%
Law of Torts Part I 100%
Law of Torts Part II 95%
Law of Torts Part III 100%
Law of Torts Part IV 100%
Criminal Law Part I 95%
Criminal Law Part II 100%
Real Property Part I 100%
Real Property Part II 95%
Real Property Part III 100%
Real Property Part IV 100%
Pleadings in Civil Action I 100%
Pleadings in Civil Action II 100%
Practice in Civil Actions 100%
Criminal Procedure 100%
Wills Part I 95%
Wills Part II 90%
Trusts 85%
Law of Private Corporations 100%
Law of Partnerships Part I 95%
Law of Partnerships Part II 100%
Constitutional Law Part I 100%
Constitutional Law Part II 95%
Constitutional Law Part III 95%
Legal Research Part I 90%
Legal Research Part II 90%
Employability Skills 100%
Ethics 100%
GRADUATING GRADE: 97.4%

Hustle, Nelly, Walt, and the rest of the guys put together a celebratory meal in honor of my graduation. I hadn't aced the course as I'd wanted to, but I did my best. My intention had been to do well in honor of my mother, and I think I did that.

The extent of Walt's involvement in the preparation of the meal, as almost always, was him saying, "get whatever food you need out of my box," as he walked briskly by on his way to the card table. I hope he doesn't mind me putting this out to the world, but he spent a lot of time…I was about to say *gambling*, but that wouldn't be strictly accurate. He played a lot of poker, but what he did couldn't really be called gambling because it's not gambling if you never lose. He might lose for one day, but much like a casino or the stock market, his overall arc was economic growth. Three steps forward, one step back, two steps forward, one step back, four steps forward, one step back…that's what we call winning in the long run. I don't know why they kept playing him. Suckers. His biggest gambling problem was finding places to put all the merchandise he won.

Walt never minded footing the bill for a meal so long as it was well-prepared and off the chain. Quality was his main concern when it came to meals.

My certification as a paralegal had been a long time coming. I'd been a jailhouse lawyer for nearly 20 years, but now I was bona fide. I showed Nelly my certificate.

"You know what this means, right?" he asked.

"What?"

"You can charge a lot more for your work now."

"Hells, yeah!" I replied. "My rates just quadrupled!"

They didn't. I charge guys only what they can afford, and only then because typewriter ribbons and typing paper are so expensive. My cost per 30 pages is $20. I charge between $1.50 to $3 per page depending on the work and the client's circumstances. And unlike some of my fellow JHLs, if I don't believe a guy has a meritorious claim I won't take his money. I'll tell him that I don't think there's anything there. They don't like to hear it, but it is what it is. Also, just like my real-world counterparts, I do a certain percentage of pro bono work every year.

My only line in the sand is that I won't do any work for pedophiles or sex offenders. Not even if what they want me to do isn't related to their case, I won't even do a Power of Attorney or an Affidavit for them. It's my prerogative.

In all seriousness, I would like to say that I learned a vast mountain of knowledge about litigation and the law from that course that I hadn't known. Before Blackstone I had no idea how much I didn't know. I highly recommend it to anyone who's serious about studying law from inside. Blackstone Career Institute. They're legit. When I get out I'd love to work as a paralegal for a prisoner rights firm who specializes in suing correctional facilities over conditions of confinement. Talk about a dream job.

The holidays were coming up fast. They would be my first without my mother. Not that the holidays in prison were ever anything special to begin with.

One thing that Walt and I had done for the holidays was had a bunch of movies donated to the institution. I love movies, always have, I've always loved the art of storytelling in comics, books, songs, and cinema. Movies are a form of escape for everyone, but even more so for those in prison. It's an enjoyment I'm sure I share with many other prisoners.

Sidenote, I learned something about storytelling by watching movies with all these different cultures and age groups. Truth and realness are what sets great storytelling apart and connects people as human beings. I watched "Slingblade" in prison in Menard. The gallery was so quiet you could hear a pin drop. Blacks, Latinos, and whites watched rapt, together.

The same thing with John Q. Hardline racist whites and Nation of Islam "Kill Whitey" black men all watched that movie together on the same gallery as quiet as mice. Truth can bridge that great divide and unite seemingly irreconcilable people, if only for a moment. That's how you know when the storytelling is great. I can only hope for a fraction of that in my own writing. I'm still at the point where I'm just hoping what I'm writing doesn't suck.

The movie situation in Jacksonville is what did suck. We were lucky if we saw one movie every two weeks, usually something from 20 years ago. "The Matrix." "Coach Carter." "The Fast and the Furious."

Straight garbola.

Our LTS (Leisure Time Services) guy, Getz, was really dropping the ball. He only had one function during the pandemic; movies. There wasn't anything else going on. There were no basketball, softball, or soccer tournaments. There wasn't a tiddlywinks tournament going on, for that matter. Movies were it.

We kept trying to catch Getz to speak to him about the bogus movie situation, but it wasn't easy because although we were walking to the chow hall again and going to and from work in the inmate commissary, we still weren't getting a whole lot of movement.

Then one day we happened to catch him on the walkway as we were returning to commissary from lunch. He was impeccably dressed in the latest designer fashions, as always, not a hair out of place. He looked like he was on his way to a photo shoot as the monthly centerfold for "Beefcake Twink Magazine."

"Man, what's up with these bogus-ass movies?" we asked.

"I know, guys, but my hands are tied by the lady in the business office," he replied. "I can only order certain movies from Netflix, and only a certain number at a time. If you want some movies, just have your family donate them. I'll show whatever they send."

"Really? What-EVER they send?"

"Don't be an idiot, Nick. I'll show whatever they send within the guidelines. You've been locked up long enough to know what that is."

The prison was already taking 25 cents out of every dollar that our families sent us and putting it into the Inmate Benefit Fund. That was where our movies were supposed to be coming from, but whatever. I ponied up the bread for the complete series of "Game of Thrones" and Walt *really* went in. He got the complete series of "Power," "Shameless," "The Corner," "West World," and like 30 or so movies. We sent the money to his girl, Shamekia, then she handled the business and sent the movies back in as donations. Bam! Just that easy. Merry Christmas, Jacksonville. You're welcome. Warden Roberson was long gone, so I was finally going to get to see the final season of "Game of Thrones."

Looking back, I have to say; it's heartbreaking to have such great anticipation for something that so badly sucked.

Big Nelly and one of our mentors, the gym rat, Ricky.

One of our participants, Savage, making cards.

KHQA ✓
3d · 🌐

AN ACT OF KINDNESS: Inmates at Jacksonville Correctional Center made cards for veterans and active military members.

Local news Facebook headline.

Ms. Briney put something together for the Level Uppers to do for the holidays. She was all about positive exposure for the program, so she had us make Christmas cards for disabled veterans and active duty service members. It was a way to keep the participants focused on positivity and give them something to do while also showing the rest of the world that not everyone in prison were low lifes. Local television media covered the event, and the story appeared on the station's Facebook page.

In the interest of full transparency, I feel I should point out the fact that, while many in prison are interested in change, there are so many more who are not. I must concede that prison does, in fact, contain people who are, in fact, low lifes. Just keeping it real. Over the years I have seen far too many men get out only to come right back to prison, often in a matter of months or weeks, sometimes days. I know one man who didn't make it 24 hours. Idiots.

It's frustrating for those of us who've been incarcerated for decades to see this scenario play out time and again when we know that we would never squander such a precious gift as freedom. It's never difficult to spot the ones who are coming back.

"So, you ready for the world?"

"Hell, yeah! I mean, you know, I'm'a still do what I do, but I'm gonna be smart about it this time. I might sell a few bags just to get back on my feet until I get a job, maybe I'll party on the weekends, do some lines, but I'm gonna be low key about it."

"Oh, dude…you're coming back to the joint."

"Man, that's some hating-ass shit to say! Why would you say that to me? You don't know that, you can't see the future. I might get out and sell drugs the rest of my life and never see another cop ever again!"

"Bro, listen to me. Just listen because I want you to get the full understanding of what I'm telling you. One thousand percent, you're coming back to the joint. Guaranteed. When it happens, I want you to think back to this conversation because it's definitely going to happen. Like, for sure."

"Fuck you, man, you don't know shit."

And then fast forward a few weeks after they get out and, sure enough, here they come. They always seem to have the same dumbass look on their faces, a sort of triple mix between disbelief, anger, and sadness. It's a very distinct expression seen on the faces of parole violators everywhere in their mug shots.

I don't understand why they do it. They must like their wives getting nailed by other dudes. Not me. When I get out, I 100 percent guarantee that I'm *never* coming back to prison. However many years, months, weeks, days, or hours I have remaining on this planet when I reach my outdate, rest assured that they will be spent basking in the magical glow of sweet, sweet freedom.

Facts, son.

CHAPTER TWENTY-SIX

Pandemic 4th Quarter

A new year was upon us; 2021 had finally arrived after one of the longest years of my entire life, as I'm sure it was for many others. Like, probably everyone. You know, if I had to guess. Then, on January 5th (the anniversary of my arrest; not a good omen as I'm now looking back), I received the perfect ending to such a year.

A letter arrived from the Illinois Prisoner Review Board. Oh my! Yeah, baby, this was IT! I signed for the letter with my heart fluttering away like I was a 13-year-old girl waiting to hear whether or not I'd made the cheer squad, then tore it open and read. My Petition for Executive Clemency has been...

...DENIED.

What...in the actual...fuck?

You've got to be kidding me. I read on. They had "thoroughly reviewed" and spent a great deal of time "carefully considering" my petition and had "not reached this decision lightly." Yeah, right. I had included the names and contact information of several IDOC employees as character references, and I later learned that the Prisoner Review Board had not contacted any of them. Not one.

As bummed out as I was about it, it was also a gut punch to several other guys who had clemency petitions pending. When Red found out, he was vocal about his feelings on the subject.

"Come on, man, if you can't get clemency, who can? Who? Tell me. I'm going to write the Board and tell 'em to just say they ain't giving out no clemencies. Just say that, then. If Nick can't get a clemency, just be real and say you ain't giving them out. Tell us that, then."

I try to be humble, but I have to admit here that I was in full agreement with Red's sentiments. It was a hard hit to take. What the hell were they looking for? I had served 22 years of a 28-year sentence. I had been promised 20 years to plead guilty. I was a military veteran with virtually no criminal history prior to my current conviction. I had a wealth of emotional and financial support available to me from family and friends. I had a release plan, places to stay, employment opportunities. I had been permanently disabled by the prison healthcare system. I had received certificates from almost everything the IDOC had to offer, I was a certified peer educator, I was a certified peer mentor, I had been in A-Grade and stayed out of trouble since 2008.

What were they looking for?

I'd taken full responsibility for my actions. I felt like I was beefing with God again. I'd networked and corresponded with two Illinois legislators. Not the right two, apparently. Into it with God.

Not where you want to be.

Renaldo Hudson, if you ever read this, just know that I got nothing but love for you. You deserve everything you have and all that your freedom still has in store for you. But in that moment, I have to be honest, I was very envious of you. Totes jelly, as the kids say. Why Naldo, Lord, and not me? How much longer are you going to hold your foot on my neck, Lord? What more do I have to do?

It took me a few days, but I came to peace with it. If this was how God wanted to play it, so be it. This is the path I have to walk, fine. What choice did I have? I could go along peacefully with God's plan, or I could go kicking at the goads and fighting God every step of the way. Either way, I was going down that path.

May as well go obediently.

With the denial of my clemency as the cap to a year that I'd begun with such optimism, a year that inflicted upon me such loss, I have to say something. Please forgive my profanity here, everyone, but this needs to be said.

2020, I am now speaking directly to you. Fuck you, 2020, you punk bitch mother fucker. Everybody hates you, and we're all glad you're gone. You're the worst. Fuck you right up your stupid ass. You can suck on a big giant dick and choke on it, 2020.

If I'm ever in a restaurant years from now, should I be so fortunate, and I order a bottle of wine and waiter comes back to the table and says, "We have a nice 2020 Rothschild red, sir," I'll probably snatch the bottle out of his hand and try to break it over his head.

2020 gets no play in my ride.

Chapter Twenty-Seven

Pandemic 4th Quarter

Time kept on slippin', slippin', slippin' into the future. Pittsfield Work Camp finally had to close when the last of their prisoners were released from their facility. Their staff came to Jacksonville. We now had the workforce of three facilities (Green County Work Camp, Pittsfield Work Camp, and Jacksonville Correctional Center) coming in to report for duty at a time when the prisoner population was well under half capacity and moving quickly to one-third capacity. There were officers everywhere and nothing for them to do. The facility was still shut down due to quarantine.

Things were slowly beginning to loosen up, though. For one thing, George Strode was finally forced to reopen the law library when enough prisoners complained. Of course, Nelly quit his inmate commissary job and went back to being the facility law clerk. He tried to get me a job there as well, but Strode and I had had some issues, so it was a no-go. He ended up getting Chavez the slot.

Level Up was in a new 10-week cycle. Buddha had decided to drop out as a mentor, which was probably for the best. Confidentiality being one of the most important aspects of our facilitation of groups (what's said in group stays in group), I'm not going to put anybody's business out there in a book. I'd be bogus for that. I'll just say that although Buddha's heart may have been in the right place, he was having trouble connecting with the participants. They didn't respond well to him. I partnered up with D4Berry for the new group cycle. We made a pretty good team, more or less.

With a vaccine rumored to be right around the corner, the biggest scam in American corrections today…oh, wait. I'm sorry. I meant to say GEO. Let's try that again. With a vaccine rumored to be right around the corner, GEO decided to restart. They had ceased operation during quarantine as had every other educational, substance abuse, mental health, and leisure activity program in the IDOC. There'd been no program activity whatsoever aside from Level Up, at least in Jacksonville. While the GEO drug counselors and the Clinical Services staff had been cowering in their offices, trembling in fear and on the verge of soiling themselves, Ms. Briney had been coming to the COVID-infested wing every day in full PPE, sitting in on groups, taking notes, and working to improve the program.

But now GEO was coming back. Can't just accept millions of dollars from the state and not come in to work. They'd been doing that for months already. A rivalry quickly developed between our two programs. GEO was big money and they liked being the only girl at the dance, so they didn't take too kindly to our rag-tag little peer mentor squad outshining them in the local media. Enmity between us was inevitable.

GEO kicked it off when they, in need of participants, acquired the Level Up participant list and used it as their candidate roster. They were attempting to fill their ranks while simultaneously erasing us from existence. Jacksonville's prisoner count was hovering just above 400, so there was definitely a shortage of inmates. The pickings were getting slim. While a few of our guys jumped ship for the time off their sentences (no hard feelings), including some of our mentors like Ricky, B, and Cardio, most of our people chose to stay.

This confused the hell out of GEO. They couldn't wrap their minds around why they didn't go. Why would they choose to stay in Level Up where they could not earn sentence credits instead of going to GEO where they <u>could</u> earn time off of their sentences? The reason was because they felt like they were getting something valuable out of our program, tools that were going to help them stay out once they got out. They felt that all GEO had to offer was an earlier outdate, which didn't mean much if you weren't ready for it.

For our new cycle we'd added new subjects like financial planning and banking, resume writing and job interview skills, career planning for people with criminal convictions, parenting skills, and more. The GEO counselors kept coming back to reinterview the Level Up guys who'd turned them down two, three, and four times.

"Are you sure you don't want to come to GEO?"

"Yes. Positive."

"But are you really sure?"

"Yes."

"But are you really, really sure?"

"If I wasn't before, I definitely am now because the way you keep sweating me about it is a little creepy. You asked, I said no. have some self-respect, move on, don't grovel, girl. It's not a good look. And before you ask again, yes, I'm sure I don't want to come to the GEO program. I've never been more sure of anything in my entire life."

Their little ploy to destroy our program hadn't been successful. They would need to come better than that, try a different tactic. See, they couldn't just outright dismantle us because Alyssa Williams, Director of Programs for the IDOC, was down with the peer mentor concept, as was our director, Rob Jeffreys. Our opponents would have to subtly undermine us in such a way that we implode from within so they could point and say, "See? It didn't work!"

I have to hand it to them, what they came up with next wasn't half bad. They moved a bunch of nonparticipants onto our wing. Not just any random guys, either. They sent us some straight up derelicts, about 35 of them.

At the height of quarantine during the Dr. Baker/Ashley Clement COVID shuffle charade when they'd been pretending that not everyone in the prison had already had coronavirus, they'd had to move nonparticipants onto the Level Up wing out of necessity. According to the fictional red zone/safe zone (reality check; the whole prison was red zone) map that they'd been going off of at the time, they had nowhere else to put them.

This latest move, however, was an act of sabotage. I know I sound paranoid saying it, but it was exactly that. Sabotage. They did it on a day when the Warden and Ms. Briney weren't at work. What the hell? Warden Scott had promised us that this wasn't going to happen again.

There was an element within Jacksonville's hierarchy (along with GEO) who did not like our peer-led program. The term "inmates leading inmates" kept getting thrown around.

At the same time, a lot of officers and other staff who'd had their doubts about our program back in the beginning were now believers. We called a mentor meeting to decide how to deal with the current crisis. There were two schools of thought. Some felt we should halt groups immediately until the issue was resolved, i.e. the NPs removed from off of our wing. They made the argument that if we didn't make a stand and let it be known that these actions wouldn't be tolerated, then the administration would think we were okay with it and keep doing it. Others felt that us halting groups and disrupting our program was exactly what our opponents wanted, and if we halted groups, we'd be allowing them to win. They insisted that we had to power through it, the same way Hustle, Chavez, Bucher, Dolla, and the others had done when the rest of the mentors had been sidelined by COVID.

The second point of view, that we should power through it, became the prevailing notion. We did just that, and in so doing we witnessed something remarkable take place.

At first, the wild boys who'd arrived met our expectations. They were a disruptive presence. Then, however, a transformation began to occur. During group sessions the dayroom would become quiet. Normally rowdy nonparticipants would sit on the outskirts of the sessions and listen in. One by one they approached mentors, catching us alone, speaking in hushed tones, their eyes darting as though they didn't want to be seen by their friends.

"Hey, um…I didn't know this program was like this. Do you think maybe I could sign up?"

Not all of them did this, but many did. Even the ones who weren't interested in signing up remained respectful of our rules and quiet during groups. Guys who were habitual IDR catchers stopped catching IDRs. Our wing was on point, easily the cleanest in the entire facility. By far. What our opponents had intended was that the rowdies would be a negative influence on our program, but the opposite occurred. We became a positive influence on them, proving that the program worked.

Unbeknownst to us at the time, Level Up gained the most unlikely of allies during this ordeal; a staff member named Lieutenant Dodds. Every prison has officers like Lieutenant Dodds, by-the-book sticklers for the rules. I know I'm probably going to catch some flack for what I'm about to write, but it's the truth, so here goes. Dodds may have had a reputation as a crank, and he may have been disliked by the entire prisoner population and even some (or more than some) of the staff, but in my 22 years of incarceration I have never minded officers such as him, and here's why.

Dodds is the same person today as he was yesterday, and he's going to be the same next week, next month, and next year. He is unyielding in his application of IDOC policies and procedures. If you're not in compliance he's going to pull your card, but by the same token, if you have something coming (by the book) then he's going to make sure you get it. He's not your buddy, your homie, or your friend. He's a correctional officer with the rank of lieutenant at the prison where you are an inmate, and that's the end of it. You know what to expect; rules and procedure. I can work with that. I'll always have just a bit of the Army in my bones for the rest of my life, and I know how to move around officers such as him.

The same standard he holds prisoners to he holds his officers to, as well. It always gets me when an inmate, say, I don't know…let's say he has his hot pot rigged to boil (a no-no) and he has it out in plain view rocking away as Dodds is coming through the rooms, then when Dodds confiscates his hot pot, the inmate will say, "Dodds is bogus! He took my pot and wrote me a ticket!"

No, dude. You're bogus. You knew Dodds was on location. You should have been a better criminal…and it just now occurs to me as I'm typing this that I've taken the side of an officer over that of a prisoner. Oh well. I stand by it.

At any rate, Dodds witnessed firsthand how our program had had a positive impact on the troublemaker prisoners exposed to it. Our program had gained a valuable ally because Dodds was an advocate whose voice carried weight within the administration.

It was a good thing, too, because a time was fast approaching when our program was going to need an ally of his caliber.

Chapter Twenty-Eight

Pandemic 4th Quarter

One of the best things about being back on our wing was being able to attend church services every Sunday. I know it may not seem like it from some of the things I say (or in this case, write), but my relationship with God is important to me, even if we do get into it from time to time.

The chapel was still closed until further notice, so we held service right in the dayroom every Sunday morning for anyone who wanted to attend. Just because chapel was closed didn't mean we couldn't worship. This was all Walt, I have to admit. He'd been conducting services throughout quarantine wherever he'd been. One thing I have to say about him, he's a man of God. Like, for real, for real. I've known Walt for years, but after a few months of being in the next bunk over from him is when I really got to know him. It's a common thing not only in prison but everywhere; you truly get to know someone when you live around them. There have been guys who were best friends for years, then when they become cellies they're ready to kill each other.

Walt had his minor vices, as do we all, but every night before he went to sleep, no matter what was going on in his life, he spent anywhere from 30 minutes to an hour in the Word of God. Now, I know the Word. I'm well familiar with it. I've read the Bible cover to cover a couple of times, the New Testament several times, completed more than a dozen Bible study correspondence courses over the years. But <u>knowing</u> the Word and staying <u>in</u> the Word are two different things. I don't stay in the Word like I should, not every day. Not like Walt. But I'm working on it.

When Walt speaks at service, one thing he always says is, "Don't think just because I'm up here and y'all are sitting over there that I have it all together. Don't think I'm better than y'all, and definitely don't put me on no pedestal. I'm just a guy with flaws and sins like everybody else who God decided to use to spread His message."

Humility aside, you can feel the Holy Spirit move when Walt speaks. His walk is real, and the world is in dire need of strong, devout men of God such as him. One look at any random news broadcast is ample evidence of this. Communities need natural leaders like him now more than ever.

The thing that happened next in the epic GEO/Level Up struggle really pissed me off. See, that's another thing about Walt; nothing ever seems to phase him. I wish I could be more like that. In all the years I've known him I can count on one hand the times I've seen him really heated. Like pissed off ready to fight, I mean. And even then, he didn't. A common exchange with Walt might go:

NICK: They sold us these hot pots a week ago and now they're changing the rule and they say we can't have these hot pots anymore! They're confiscating them! Why aren't you more pissed off about this?

WALT: Whatever.

Dang it! Not going to lie, there have been times when his lack of anger was a factor that made me angry. That's called irony. But back to the latest GEO/Level Up squabble.

Lincoln Land College read the interview that Ms. Briney, Nelly, and myself had done for the Jacksonville Courier. They had loved the article, thought our program was great, and wanted to get involved with Level Up.

Here's a copy of the article.

Peer Program Teaches Life After Prison
Those nearing release learn skills to help return to life outside
Samantha McDanial-Ogletree
Published 4:26 a.m. CDT, Monday, August 3, 2020

A program in its infancy at the Jacksonville Correctional Facility will be focusing on helping those soon to be released develop life skills that will help them as they reintegrate into society.

The Illinois Department of Corrections facility is implementing Level Up: Better Than Before, a peer mentoring program that will focus on teaching the participants various skills prior to the end of their sentence.

Rochelle Briney, a corrections specialist and the program coordinator, said the program is just starting and in the early stages of development with the first class of 17 mentors just receiving their certification.

Briney said the mentors are all volunteers and were selected by staff members based on their behavior and character.

"They went through 40-plus hours of training to become mentors," Briney said. "They have really good character and their behavior is high standard. They help reinforce positive behavior among their peers."

The program will include six sessions a day lead by the mentors. The mentors will each lead small groups of 10 throughout the day on their wing. The topics will include anger management, life skills, relationship skills, leadership, mindfulness, overcoming criminal thinking, and conflict resolution.

While modeled after similar programs, the Jacksonville program is being modified to fit the needs of the participants and will continue to be developed.

"We hope to add more topics and programs," said Nicholas Chittick, one of the mentors of the program.

While there are currently enough topics for each participant to do two 10-week phases, there is potential for a third phase for a full 30-week program.

For Chittick, the program is a chance for him to help send good back out into the community through those that are being released.

"You can look at prison like a factory. You can export positivity or negativity. This program is a way to export positivity. We want to give them a chance not to come back to this spot."

Arnell Williams, another mentor for the program, said the goal of the program is to help those serving time develop the skills they'll need as they reenter society.

"We are hoping to better ourselves and the people around us," Williams said.

"This sends them back to society with skill sets they can use to become productive members of society. We want to help foster positive behavior."

Williams said he volunteered to be a mentor because a lot of people in his wing already look to him for advice.

Both Williams and Chittick have been serving time for more than 20 years, and both want others to avoid repeating offenses and ending up back in jail.

"If I can help a guy learn from his mistakes early, to help him not come back here, I feel I am leading a purposeful life," Chittick said.

While the focus is on those that will be leaving prison within a two-year period, Briney said they have to be willing to participate as well.

"We are teaching them that they have to be an active participant in their own rehabilitation," Briney said. "When they go h ome, we want them to be successful in their own communities."

Lincoln Land wanted to help Level Up by providing additional learning opportunities for our participants. A representative from their school contacted Ms. Briney and pitched her an idea for a pilot program. It was a proposal that they would provide training to the mentors to become GED tutors. Once trained and certified by Lincoln Land College we would help our program participants study and prepare to take their GED tests for those who did not already have GEDs. Lincoln Land would then provide accredited GED testing when the participants were ready.

This was remarkable for a couple of reasons. First, schools who approach the IDOC always do so with their hand out. They all want that gravy train contract money from the state. Lincoln Land, by contrast, was offering to provide funding and resources TO the state as opposed to being yet another vulture suckling at the teat of the Illinois taxpayer.

Secondly, the reason they wanted to do this was because of the interview we'd done. A little positive publicity goes a long way. You may find this hard to believe, but media coverage of prisons and prisoners isn't always positive. Level Up was shining bright, bringing positive exposure and new educational opportunities to the prisoners incarcerated there. Ms. Briney happily set up a meeting with the representative, scheduling a time for them to come to the facility in order to discuss their ideas in person and in greater detail.

On the day of the meeting Ms. Briney was excited about the prospects of what lie ahead, as were we all. She decided to go up to the employee commissary that morning for a coffee, something she rarely did. It was a good thing she did on this particular occasion a coworker saw her and asked, "Aren't you going to the meeting with the Lincoln Land College rep today?"

"Yes, it's this afternoon," Ms. Briney replied.

"No, they changed it. They didn't tell you? Van Winkle and Warden Augie are going to meet her now, she just got on grounds."

Van Winkle, you'll remember, was the head of Clinical Services. Or at least the figure head. In practice, Ms. Delaney ran Clinical Services. Both of them were all about GEO, and neither was a fan of Level Up. It was widely rumored that Van Winkle suffered a very severe premature ejaculation problem as well as being afflicted with an abnormally small penis. Allegedly. I have no firsthand knowledge of this, nor do I want any.

Ms. Briney arrived at the conference room just as the meeting was getting ready to begin, seating herself across the table from Van Winkle as his face dropped in visible disappointment at her arrival. Introductions were made, pleasantries were exchanged, and the Lincoln L and rep made her pitch.

"What we have in mind is pretty simple, really," she said. "We want to train your guys as GED tutors, and then…"

"Let me stop you right there," Van Winkle said. "With the COVID restrictions we have in place, that's not going to happen here. Not any time soon."

"Oh, we've been made aware of the COVID guidelines by Rochelle. We intend to conduct the training remotely, via Zoom."

"Yeah…that's not going to work. We're just not set up for anything like that here."

"Sure we are," Ms. Briney interjected. "We have computers in our classrooms that have internet access, and we have large flat screen TVs we can place in front of the class."

"Oh, great," said Van Winkle as he ground his teeth, staring daggers at Ms. Briney. "Good for you. We'll have to wait and see, I'll have to talk to the GEO counselors and see if they even want to do this, and then, if they do, how we would go about implementing it."

"GEO?" the rep asked, puzzled. "No, we wanted to work with the prisoners in the Level Up: Better Than Before peer mentoring program that we read about."

"Oh, no, no, no," Van Winkle replied. "That's absolutely out of the question. That thing hasn't even been going, it got shut down right at the beginning of quarantine like everything else."

"What do you mean?" asked Ms. Briney. "Level Up has been functioning continuously ever since it began."

"But...I thought...it has?"

"Yes. In fact, they're the only program that has been functioning throughout the pandemic."

This is a good example of the lack of communication at Jacksonville. At least once or twice a week officers or other staff would walk through our wing and go, "What are all these chairs and books for? Is this some kind of honor dorm?"

"This is the Level Up wing."

"What the hell is Level Up?"

This continued happening months and months after our program had been rolling. The left hand doesn't know what the right hand is doing. That's the IDOC in a nutshell.

"Well, regardless of that," Van Winkle continued, "There's no way they're going to allow prisoners to act as tutors."

"Of course they will, they already do," Ms. Briney insisted. "We have inmate peer educators, teacher assistants, peer mentors...we have a prisoner down here who was teaching music theory before the pandemic."

She was talking about me! Yay!

The animosity between Van Winkle and Ms. Briney was growing uncomfortably obvious to everyone in the room. Warden Augie sat as silent as a stone. He was at Jacksonville to quietly ride out the remainder of his time before his retirement and pension. He wasn't about to get involved in any inner departmental conflict. And just for my homie who was just reading over my shoulder and had something to say, no, it's not interdepartmental conflict, because that would be a conflict between two departments. Ms. Briney and Van Winkle were both in Clinical Services, so it's an <u>inner</u> departmental conflict. Grammar lesson over, now stop reading over my shoulder.

That was for him, not you guys. That's what's wrong with prison today. Too many nosy people who don't mind their own business. And now back to our regularly scheduled programming already in progress.

Where was I?

Oh yeah.

The Lincoln Land rep chimed in to try and smooth over the ever-building tension in the room.

"The prisoners wouldn't be teachers, they would simply help their fellow inmates study for the test, that's all. The testing would be administered under the supervision of an approved member of our faculty or other approved delegate. And GEDs are just the beginning. Further down the road we'd like to add more educational opportunities for your participants. We believe that education is the key to success for everyone."

"Well, for something like this we'd have to get approval from the Educational Director of the IDOC in Springfield," said Van Winkle.

"Okay," the rep replied. "How do we make that happen?"

"We don't. I'm going to be completely honest with you. I don't think now is a time when the department is looking to provide funding for anything like what you're describing. Frankly, the state is looking to save money right now, not spend it."

"Oh, you misunderstand me. We aren't looking for funding, we're going to provide the funding and all the necessary materials and resources."

A look of utter bewilderment came over Van Winkle's face.

"But…I mean…I don't under…why would you do that?" he asked. The notion of a school not looking for funding was so alien to him he could not have been more surprised had she suggested they take off all their clothing and ride around the prison grounds on bicycles.

"We would do it because we believe in what we read. We want to be a part of making our community better, just as the Level Up program strives to do. So, how do we get approval from the Educational Director?"

"I can call Springfield today and…" the warden began to say before Van Winkle cut him off.

"Shut up, warden, you're not calling anyone," Van Winkle snapped.

"Okay. Okay. I understand."

"I'll send an email to…" started Ms. Briney before she was interrupted.

"No, no, no, no, no! Let's everybody just calm the fuck down for a minute!" He got in the warden's face. "Nobody's calling Springfield!" He turned to Ms. Briney, veins bulging, eye twitching. "Nobody's emailing the Educational Director! No one is bothering anyone in Springfield about any of this! I'll look into it myself and I'll tell you what I find out in a few months. That's it. Meeting adjourned!"

Van Winkle stood up and kicked the warden's chair.

"Get up, we're leaving, warden!"

"Okay. Okay. I understand."

Ms. Briney and the rep sat stunned. What kind of meeting had this been? Nothing had been accomplished. The warden stepped through the door of the conference room and was gone. Van Winkle followed behind but paused just before leaving and turned to address Ms. Briney and the rep.

"One more thing," he said. "I just wanted to make sure that you gals know I have a pretty severe premature ejaculation problem, and a VERY small penis," he said, then was gone.

All right. Full disclosure, I wasn't actually there for the meeting, and I don't know that Van Winkle actually said that last part. Then again, I don't know that he didn't say it, either. And also, I'm sure he didn't go in on Warden Augie as I described. Let's call it dramatic license.

"That's fucked up, Nick. You shouldn't do that."

Do what?

"Make shit up like that. This is supposed to be a nonfiction book. You'll fuck up your credibility, what little of it you have."

Um…who is this, and what are you doing in my book?

"I'm you. Only I'm real you, not the fake-ass filtered funhouse mirror version of yourself that you've been perpetrating all through this punk-ass book. I'm real Nick, and what I'm doing here is keeping your square-ass in check because you're acting fake as hell right now."

What are you talking about? I'm keeping this book 100 percent real deal Holyfield.

"Nope! That! That right there, you don't talk like that, you're an old-ass white dude from Cocoa Beach, Florida. Totes cray cray? Real deal Holy field? You need to cut it out. And that other bullshit, too."

What bullshit?

"What the hell were we talking about, idiot? That last part about the meeting. You weren't there for that, you made that whole part up. Sitting here calling this thing a nonfiction book and you're pulling some straight John Grisham shit."

Fuck John Grisham.

"Yeah, yeah...I know. <u>Fetching Raymond</u>. So, John Grisham hates jailhouse lawyers who fancy themselves musicians...that's not the point, dumbass. The point is you should only write about the things you saw with your own eyes. Dramatic license my ass. It's called lying."

Hey, man, all that shit happened. Van Winkle changing the meeting, him playing defense on Lincoln Land hooking up with Level Up, him trying to steer them to GEO, all that, Ms. Briney said so.

"Oh, did she now? Well, isn't that special! Her name's Rochelle, you stupid fuck, why do you keep calling her Ms. Briney like she's your kindergarten teacher or something? Creepy as fuck! I told you, motherfucker, ONLY WRITE WHAT YOU SAW if you want to keep it real, like you say."

I am keeping it real.

"Yeah? I see you left out the parts where you have to see mental health services once a month for all your fucked up mental issues. Where's that chapter at?"

If you're gonna tell it, tell it right. They suspended mental health services for quarantine, so I wasn't seeing anybody! Besides, that's my personal business.

"Whatever, Nicker. You never mentioned your mental health not one time, and during quarantine you damn near went through a psychotic break a couple of times. You can front to those dudes around you, but you can't front to me. I'm Real Nick. Keep getting lippy and I'll put all our business out there. Try me, motherfucker."

Go ahead. I ain't got nothing to hide.

"Oh no? Okay, bitch. Check this out, people, this motherfucker right here watches girls' high school volleyball!"

Bullshit! One time, and I thought it was college!

"Yeah, for the first 30 seconds maybe, but when you figured out what it was you kept watching. If you're gonna tell it, tell it right. Ain't that what you just said to me?"

By the time I realized what it was I was already invested in the game. I wanted to see who was gonna win. I'm a sports fan.

"Yeah, right. Sports fan. Invested in the game. I know what you were invested in, the little young blonde bitch you kept staring at."

First of all, I wasn't staring at anybody. I was watching a game. Second of all, if I was staring at anyone—which I definitely wasn't—they were probably 18, so it's okay.

"Man, no way in hell that chick was 18. And even if she was, so what? You're 52 years old, you fucking creep!"

Well, what do you expect? She looked exactly like Barbi Giovari.

"A-HA, so you WERE staring at her! I know who she looked like bitch, I'm the real Nick. I'm the one who was banging Barbi's brains out in her bedroom after school. You were the one sitting with her and her parents at the dinner table pretending to be a nice guy."

I'm real enough.

"Yeah? Then how come you don't talk about the fact that no one in your family will have anything to do with you? Brothers or sisters, nieces or nephews, aunts or uncles…not even your own sons. I notice you conveniently left all that out."

Because that's my personal baggage and it's not relevant to the story I'm trying to tell.

"It's relevant to the fact that you're a piece of shit. How about Karyn? Should we talk about her?"

Leave our wife out of this.

"No, let's don't, because you already brought her up. Earlier when you spoke of her you implied that you weren't together anymore because you were in prison. But the truth is she divorced your sorry ass years before you came to prison."

Drop it.

"No can do, buddyroo. You treated her like garbage. Hey readers, would you like to see a scene from Nick's past? See what kind of father and husband this guy was? See what kind of a true asshole wrote these words you're reading right now?"

Nobody wants to see that.

"Well, they're gonna."

SCENE
INTERIOR-NIGHT
A small Chicago apartment is dark and quiet. The camera pans across a wall of family photos then rests on a clock that reads 3:48 a.m. then continues to pan into a child's bedroom where a five-year-old boy sleeps. In the corner there is a crib with a baby asleep in it.

The camera pans out to the front door. Keys can be heard jingling then the lock clicks and the door opens. Twenty-four-year-old Nick steps into the front room carrying a guitar case. He has clearly been drinking.

Nick sets the guitar case down, takes a small baggie of white powder from the pocket of his leather jacket, then sticks his house key into the baggie and brings a small pile of white powder to his nose and sniffs.

A light goes on and Karyn emerges into the living room. She looks as though she has been crying.

KARYN: Shh! You're going to wake the boys. What time is it? Are you drunk?

NICK: (ignoring her question) Hey baby girl! You should have heard us tonight, we killed it.

KARYN: I told you, be quiet. It's the middle of the night.

NICK: (grabbing her around the waist) C'mon, don't be like that. Come here, let's have some fun.

KARYN: (pushing Nick away) Don't touch me! You think you can just come in like this whenever you want like I'm your toy. Is that all I am to you? A fuck?

Karyn moves away from Nick. He draws close, taking her face softly into his hands.

NICK: No way, how you say that? You're so much more than that. You know that, right?

KARYN: (her face softens, she looks into his eyes) I am?

NICK: Yeah, sweetness. You're way more than just a fuck to me. I mean, you give head too, but we ain't gotta go into all that right now 'cause you ain't that good at it.

KARYN: (pushing Nick) Motherfucker!

NICK: (laughing) Fuck this, I'm out of here.

Nick stagers out the door, slamming it behind him. The baby starts to cry. Karyn slings the door open.

KARYN: (calling after Nick) Don't come back, motherfucker! Don't come back!

END SCENE

"Nice way to treat our wife."

Fuck you, that was probably you. You're real Nick, right?

"I'm real enough to beat your ass."

Bring it, bitch motherfucker!

A008f94J5=J+)#@!D

D/mn it, I just punched my typewriter keyboard. No w/y, I think I broke it. I'll h/ve to t/ke / bre/k and pick this up ag/in l/ter.

I'm going through some things right now.

CHAPTER TWENTY-NINE

Pandemic 4th Quarter

How do you want to do this? I think the best thing would be to just pretend that my little meltdown in the last chapter never happened. In my experience the best thing to do whenever something unpleasant or traumatic happens in your life is to bury it way down deep inside and never, ever speak of it again. Ever.

That's probably the most healthy option. Hmm. Wonder if that lifelong policy has anything to do with my present-day health issues? Nah.

The clock continued to tick and tock. I finally received my Merit Review from the U.S. District Court. They dismissed seven of my 10 defendants, claiming that I had failed to outline sufficient facts to sustain claims against them. See, that's what they do in the federal court. In order to keep initial pleadings brief they issue specific guidelines to pro se prisoners stating that their filings be succinct and outline only the most basic, relevant facts. They do so for their own benefit and even provide these short fill-in-the-bank formatted Civil Complaints that we're supposed to use.

Then, when you follow their guidelines, they dismiss claims or defendants, if not your entire case, because you didn't go into enough detail. Many judges believe, wrongly, that prisoners just sit around dreaming up frivolous lawsuits. It comes from a faulty assumption, the same way judges erroneously state that prisons provide for a prisoner's basic needs, therefore they have less need of money than people who are free when they deny prisoner petitions to proceed in forma pauperis (as a poor person).

An oft-cited case in the 7th Circuit (Illinois jurisdiction) is Maboneza v. Kincaid. It held that courts have broad discretion in assessing a prisoner's poverty because prisons provide them with food, clothing, shelter, and medical care. Put aside that most prisoner lawsuits (like mine) are brought in regards to the fact that prisons DON'T provide adequate medical care, Maboneza is yet based on flawed presumptions.

In the IDOC prisoners are responsible for purchasing their own soap, deodorant, toothpaste, toothbrush, laundry detergent, socks, boxer shorts, t-shirts, bedsheets, pillows, gym shoes (70 bucks a pop or more) or any of the other myriad necessary sundries not provided by the state. Upon entry into the IDOC a prisoner is provided with two pairs of blue uniform pants (used) and two button-up or pullover blue shirts (also used). That's it. All of the above listed items are considered luxuries and not necessary. I'm sure that if they're pressed they'll claim that the above items are passed out to every prisoner on a weekly basis. I'm here to tell you, in the real world it is NOT the case.

And food. Thanks to our previous Governor Rod Blagojevich we were switched over to farm-feed-grade soy in our diets for nearly two decades. The boxes coming in were actually stamped FOR PRISONER CONSUMPTION ONLY. Now, when I first got to prison we were fed real food. It may not have always been prepared all that great, but it was real potatoes on your tray, not reconstituted potato powder. We got real beef, real pork, real chicken. Fresh oranges, apples, bananas and salad every day, twice a day. Blago put a stop to all that. We don't get of that anymore. Everything is soy, powdered, and canned, with the exception of eggs. Occasionally (perhaps once every one or two months) we'll get an apple or an orange.

When I was newly imprisoned, another difference from then and now is in the prisoners themselves. Back then you didn't see anyone using walkers and canes. Sixty-five- and 70-year-old men were on the weight pile, slim, cut up to death, and pushing up 300 pounds on the bench.

"Damn, grandpa! Let me stay out of your way!"

Now you have 40- and 50-year-olds, guys who work out religiously (like me) who can barely walk and have guts that stick one or two feet from their bodies. Over the past 20 years since Blago pulled that stunt there has been an explosion of type II diabetes and all sorts of other health problems in the IDOC, and I know in my heart and soul that our diets are the reason why. Prison chow in its present form is poison.

Inmate commissary food isn't much better but it's the only alternative. I'm currently on the keto diet (I read that it's good for neurologic maladies) and I buy tuna, summer sausage, sunflower seeds, mackerel, shredded chicken, shredded beef, roast beef, shredded pork, pork bacon, powdered eggs, pepperoni slices, pickles, hamburgers, Velveeta block cheese, Velveeta cup cheese, peanuts, jalapenos, and all the other keto-friendly stuff I can off the inmate commissary, and I avoid the chow hall like the plague. Now that I can afford it, I have been to the inmate chow hall perhaps six or seven times this year. And it's late July. It's working. I'm getting better, but I spend about $400 a month on food or more. But according to Maboneza the prison provides all of my food.

Unhealthy food that poses a danger to my wellbeing.

In Jacksonville we're even responsible for paying for our own ID clips, and they're part of our uniform, so we have to buy them.

As far as the court's erroneous belief that prisoners just sit around dreaming up frivolous lawsuits, I mean, I'm sure there are frivolous lawsuits. In my experience, however, the vast majority of prisoners who have legitimate claims; prisoners who are severely beaten without justification, who are denied or delayed critical medical care with horrific results, or who are denied due process rights by prison officials that have the nonchalant arrogance of people who know they will never be held accountable, these prisoners never bother to file claims because they know that most prison lawsuits (somewhere above 90%) are dismissed. There are judges who have a record of not only failing to ever allow a prisoner lawsuit to proceed before them, but who have never once granted a pro se motion (save for procedural motions) in their entire careers.

And if a prisoner does somehow manage to beat the odds and prevail in court, prisoner damage awards are typically pennies on the dollar of what a free person might receive for the same injuries. This is primarily due to an evil law called the Prison Litigation Reform Act (PLRA). Passed in the 1990s, this so-called law severely restricted prisoners' rights to seek relief in the courts, and it makes it much easier for prisons and jails to violate prisoner rights with almost total immunity.

Earlier I mentioned the officer who told his coworker that, "Prison is the one place where you can still treat a nigger like a nigger." What people fail to realize is that the U.S. District court, using the PLRA, is striving to ensure that prison remains that one place.

At any rate, I wasn't about to go out like a punk. I amended my original complaint with pages and pages of detailed facts outlining sufficient claims against all my defendants, then refiled my suit along with a Motion to File an Amended Complaint (technically it's called a Petition for Leave to File an Amended Complaint, but this isn't a law class). It was granted. As of this writing I'm still waiting on my second Merit Review where I will find out whether my case will move forward in whole or in part.

Fingers crossed.

In my work life I reached the limits of my tolerance. One day I was putting some things into my personal bucket when Burmflailed came by.

"What's this?" he asked.

"Oh, this is my stuff," I replied. "I'm shopping later this week."

He reached into my bucket and pulled out a shredded beef pack. "Um, we're out of shredded beefs, so why do you have…it looks like six of them in your bucket?"

"Because I'm buying them. I put them in my crate before we ran out."

"No, no, no, we're not doing this. Put these shredded beefs back on the shelf. If we're out of something whenever you shop that's just tough shit for you. You're not going to be putting a bunch of stuff up so you get everything you want on your shop day. You're not special."

"Well," I thought to myself, "then why the fuck am I working over here?" I didn't know what the hell he was talking about. Of course that's how it's supposed to go. That's how it's worked in every inmate commissary in the IDOC since forever, including Jacksonville.

Working in commissary was not easy for me. Even on a goo day when I didn't do anything I was in constant pain. But with the constant bending and twisting of my back, I was in such excruciating pain that I couldn't sleep at night, and I could barely walk. Still, I could have dealt with that because I'm a bad dude. What I wasn't going to do, however, was put up with the constant pain AND Ms. B and Mr. Brinnfolled. Life is much too short.

I quit the next day.

I turned 52 on March 23, 2021. We'd been on quarantine for a year. When was this going to be over?

I'd no sooner had that thought when on March 25, 2021, the Illinois National Guard came to Jacksonville with the gift of normalcy on the horizon; the Moderna COVID vaccine. Yes! In an effort to persuade prisoners to take the vaccine, Warden Scott promised that the journey back to the "before time" would begin once most of us were vaccinated. Masks could be dispensed with. Visits would resume. School would be reopened. Church services would return, as would AA and NA. Gym and yard would return to full rotation.

It sounded good but didn't exactly work out that way.

Still, most prisoners took the vaccine. Even then, though, there were a few prisoners and most of the officers who cried about not wanting to take the vaccine, this is America, you can't force me, whatever. All the same rhetoric you hear today.

And they're right. They have a right not to get vaccinated. But if they think they have a right to not get vaccinated AND go out in public to restaurants, grocery stores, movie theaters, and planes while they're a risk factor of spreading a deadly disease to those around them and people I love, nope. That's a right they DON'T have. Now your choice is affecting others.

You have a right in America to get as drunk as you'd like in the privacy of your own home. But you don't have the right to get drunk and go drive around. No one can prove you're going to kill someone if you drive drunk. You might not. But you're still not allowed to do it.

If you're not vaccinated and you go walking around a crowded park, you might not kill anyone. But you're still a risk. You're driving drunk. It's the same thing. So, if you want to stay home, don't go out in public or to work, by all means. Don't get vaccinated. But you can't have both. At least that's how I see it.

But then, what do I know?

CHAPTER THIRTY

Pandemic 4ᵗʰ Quarter

With the vaccine administered, Jacksonville set its sights on returning to normal operations. That meant that they would resume legitimate compliance checks and shakedowns again, which they had been pencil whipping (filling out the shakedown slips, but not actually performing the shakedowns) throughout the pandemic. There'd been a lot of aspects of security that the guards had been overlooking.

An announcement was made that on April 1ˢᵗ the party was going to be over. Shakedowns and legitimate, full-scale compliance checks would reboot to maximum power. Our time of free passes was coming to an end, but hopefully so would all the restrictions we'd been living under. Maybe we'd get to see our families and friends on contact visits, maybe other privileges would return.

As things turned out, petty rule enforcement bordering on harassment returned long before our privileges did. As of this writing many of our privileges have yet to be reinstated or reinstated fully, and whether they ever will be remains uncertain.

At any rate, word around the camp was that on April 1st it was back to life, back to reality. This news came around the same time that Warden Scott retired. We were getting a new warden. Again, Warden Augie would still be the #2, but Scott was out.

I told you, warden is a very transitory position.

I'd been in Jacksonville for less than two years and had seen four wardens; Plunk, Roberson, Scott, and now Cherryl Hinthorne. I knew Hinthorne, I'd worked for her as a cook in Galesburg back when she'd been a young dietary supervisor. Hmmm. I really want to say something else right now, but I don't think I'm going to. On the record I'll say that Warden Hinthorne is a consummate professional highly deserving of the position she's been given, despite the fact that she'd just dismantled the peer mentor program at Illinois River Correctional Center from whence she came. And that's all I have to say about her. Nothing at all about her past conduct.

Ouch, that hurt!

And now I have a new scar on my tongue from biting it.

A couple of days before April 1st an incident occurred. A lieutenant came to the housing unit at about 8 a.m. He came into Room 10 and made an announcement.

"Listen up, guys, we're about to do a practice run for these upcoming compliance checks. This is to help you guys get ready and to help us get ready. You know the drill, you have to have all your stuff put up. We're not taking anything today, but this will let you know what you need to work on for when the real thing starts back up."

Okay, fine. I sat up and swung my feet over the edge of my bunk, groggy. I'd only just gotten to sleep a couple of hours ago. Walt, Nelly, and Chavez weren't in the room, they'd gone to work. Nelly had gotten Chavez a job in the library.

A few officers came into our room. Officer White, a larger gal, came straight to Walt's corner bunk with a rookie I'd never seen before on her heels, probably one of the work camp C/Os. She was wearing gloves. Why was she wearing gloves for a practice run?

"I'm gonna need a garbage bag over here," White called out. "This guy has all kinds of stuff. Look here along the wall, extra gym shoes, rolls of tissue…is that a laundry bag full of chips? Jesus, how many bags of Doritos is that?" She turned to the young rookie. "Pull this bunk out so we can bag up all this guy's stuff bagged up and take it to the Dumpster."

The rookie moved to lift Walt's bunk. It started to shift, moving perhaps an inch, when I quickly stood up. I nearly fell over. Because of my spinal damage, it takes my right leg several moments in the morning before it's strong enough to hold my body weight. I put my hand out on the corner of Walt's bunk to catch myself. What it looked like, however, was that I'd stood up and slammed Walt's bunk back up against the wall in defiance of their intentions. White and the rookie stepped back, startled, eyes wide. I went with it.

"Y'all ain't taking nothing from over here. First of all, that's commissary tissue. He paid for that. Second of all, he ain't even here, he's at work. Third of all, this ain't even a real compliance check, the lou just told us this is a practice run."

"I'm not doing no practice run," said White. "If I have to be over here, I'm doing it for real."

"Not over here you ain't."

Another officer at the front of the room spoke up, addressing White.

"The lieutenant did say that if they're at school they get a pass," he remarked.

"Well, he's at work," I said, my hand still on Walt's bunk.

"We'll see about this," said White, then stormed off in an angry huff, acting all butt-hurt about it, the rookie following.

Nelly and Chavez had seen the caravan of C/Os headed to our housing unit from inside the library and had promptly returned. Hustle, who had witnessed my stand, gave me a look of approval from across the way. Meanwhile, other officers were confiscating property in other rooms, despite what the lieutenant had said.

The lieutenant came back into Room 10. C/O White stood in the doorway watching.

"What's the problem in here?" he asked. He was looking directly at me.

"Your officers are confiscating property after you told us this was a practice run," I said.

"Well, technically they can confiscate any property not put away during a compliance check," he replied.

"Yeah, we know, but that's not what you just said. Look, lou, we ain't got no problem being in compliance, but with all due respect it's 8 o'clock in the morning. Compliance checks are at 7 o'clock, before count time, before guys have left for school and work. That's the AD [Administrative Directive] on compliance checks, and I know you know that. If you're going to enforce the rules you should follow the rules. Where are our weights? Where's our visits? We haven't seen our families in a year."

"The rules are whatever we say they are, and we'll do compliance checks whenever we feel like it, and I'm not here to listen to your fucking complaints," he said. Now I know why they called him Lieutenant Snake. It was all adding up.

That pissed me off. I'd addressed him respectfully and outlined genuine concerns, and he'd responded by basically telling me to fuck off. I was thinking of how I should reply when Nelly jumped into the fray.

"You're not here to listen to our complaints? We're not here to listen to that dumbass shit you just said either, but we got to," he said. Nelly was heated, as we all were. It wasn't even the compliance check that was at issue. It was a year of quarantine frustration boiling over into that particular moment in time. Everything we'd endured, everything we'd been denied. Six prisoners had died and counting.

More officers came into the room, crowding in. Now it was like they were trying to intimidate us, but that only escalated everyone's anger more. Chavez spoke up next.

"Hey, uh…check this out, lou. We aren't trying to be bogus, but y'all are nitpicking at us with this petty shit with this bootleg-ass compliance check, meanwhile we ain't getting nothing we're supposed to be getting. The food in this inmate chow hall we can't even eat, shit's bogus as fuck, and you don't feed us enough to fill a squirrel. My kids eat more than what we get on those trays, while at the same time you motherfuckers are going over there on staff side feasting like it's your last meal every day! I see y'all over there, every day boneless chicken breasts, bananas, oranges, apples, exclusive-ass shit. You motherfuckers got jobs, why are you eating up all the food we're supposed to be getting? Keeping us locked up in a box for a year, how much of this shit do you think we're going to take?"

Chavez was on a rant, geeking himself up to get angrier with each passing sentence. Anger was escalating. A C/O approached Hustle.

"Hey, go calm Chavez down," said the officer.

"Fuck that," said Hustle. "I agree with everything he's saying, y'all motherfuckers need to hear this shit."

The tension in the room was building. I've felt that tension before. The air had a thickness to it, as if you were to push on it the air might push back. It always gets that way just before something bad happens. It would not have taken much to tip the scale at that point. There were far more prisoners than C/Os and the prisoners were all angry. And it was the most dangerous type of anger to the security of any prison; righteous anger born of unfair treatment where the prisoners believed they were in the right. People will do extreme things when they believe they are in the right.

It's easy to say now that there was never any real danger of anything violent happening, but I'm here to tell you…in that moment we were all on the verge of something. It would not have been pretty. And just look at a guy like Nelly or Chavez or Dolla. Nelly and Dolla were pushing up 435 pounds on the bench press, and not one time, but doing repetitions with it. Squatting 500 pounds. Freakish strength. The C/Os would not have been able to do anything with them, and in that moment, had any one of us made a move, all would have followed suit. It was a room full of old-school convicts who followed a code. Well, for the most part.

Thank God that there was a person working at Jacksonville that day by the name of Sergeant Roberts. It was fortunate for everyone that he came into the room.

I don't remember exactly what he said, but I do remember that it was the best de-escalation that I've ever seen. Where the lieutenant had said, "Fuck you guys," Sergeant Roberts spoke with respect, listened to what we had to say, and sympathized.

"I know this is a bogus situation for all of us, guys, and we don't want to be here doing this any more than you guys want to be going through it, but those decisions are made way over our heads. If I could give you your weights back today, I would," he said, or words to that effect.

The lieutenant and the other officers left the room with Sergeant Roberts guarding their retreat. He even cracked a joke on his way out.

"Jesus, I thought this was supposed to be the mentor room," he said quietly, under his breath. We didn't laugh at the time (too soon) but we laughed about it later amongst ourselves.

He had expertly defused a very tense situation. I don't know what may have happened in an alternative universe, but I do know that thanks to Sergeant Robert's professionalism, we'll never know.

Interesting side note about that day, Walt had a ghost celly who never said a word. I mentioned earlier that Walt was virtually unbeatable at the poker table. This created the problem for him of excess property. What to do when you have more than double what will fit inside your property box? Not a bad problem to have, but still…a problem.

Walt's solution was very creative. During COVID, with all the prisoners coming and going, Nelly had first invented the community box. An extra property box, belonging to no one, moved around the room under various bunks that had been shaken down for that weak, was kept for Nelly and Hustle's extra property, and perhaps others in the room who required storage for chips, foodstuffs, or whatnot. It had thus far gone unnoticed.

Walt built upon this concept by creating a ghost celly. He acquired an empty property box and put it under his bunk. Then he put a mattress into the top bunk, which had been empty ever since Ricky had went over to the dark side; GEO. Walt put sheets on the mattress, put some items on the top shelf like a fan, a coffee cup, and a notebook and pen, and voila! An extra box for all his merch. It helped, but it still wasn't enough. He still needed to put stuff in other people's boxes, mine included. Random things like boxes of apple pies, for instance.

No C/O ever noticed it. They just don't pay attention to that. During count they tally bodies, not bunks. Walt's ghost celly was there on the morning of the previously described compliance check, totally unnoticed. In the coming weeks, during other compliance checks, staff would even make comments.

"Hey, you guys need to look at bunk 16. Now that's how you're supposed to keep your area. Perfect. Where is this guy?"

"Oh, he's floating around the joint somewhere. I think he's at work," I would say.

"Well, tell him to keep up the good work," they'd reply.

"Yeah, okay."

To do that I'd have needed a Ouija board.

CHAPTER THIRTY-ONE

Pandemic 4th Quarter

Level Up began another 10-week cycle. My partner, DeBerry, was about to go home, so for the new cycle I partnered up with Nelly. Finally, a partner I didn't have to carry. I could sit back and relax a little. The ironic part is that he probably thought the same thing. We were told that church services would be coming back in late April but in limited capacity. School had already reopened a few weeks prior, also in limited capacity.

With church set to reopen, Walt and I would finally be able to play the brand new music equipment that had come in more than a year ago. Unfortunately, we were only able to do this a couple of times before Van Winkle hit Level Up with a right cross worthy of Mike Tyson.

Pittsfield Work Camp was set to reopen. They needed bodies, and Van Winkle was in charge of the transfer list. He placed virtually all of the mentors on the list, certainly the ones who mattered, at least. Nelly, Hustle, Walt, Dolla, Chavez, Shakur (a new mentor, but a good one), myself…it was a death blow to the program. Many of our participants were also placed on the list.

Walt and I were slated for the first thing on wheels out of Jacksonville, but I was restricted from being transferred due to a medical hold, which meant that I wasn't going anywhere. I was scheduled for outside specialist medical appointments due to all of my health problems. I don't normally talk in detail about this stuff because it's pretty embarrassing, but hey, I've been pretty relentless against the powers that be. Turnabout is fair play.

Not to make it all about me, but I want you to try and understand that throughout every experience I've written about, including as I sit here typing these words, I was in constant, ceaseless pain. In my younger days I could never fathom how anyone would ever think of killing themselves, but now I get it. I only recently became aware of the existence of a drug called Neurontin, specifically designed to alleviate nerve damage pain. Yeah, they won't give it to me, but man does it sound great.

My bowels are basically paralyzed. Sluggish, the Wexford people call it. I'm on every kind of laxative there is; Lactalose, Miralax, Dulcoset, Fiberlax. My bladder won't empty, the urologist found that it's retaining a crazy amount of milliliters of urine post urination. They haven't said, but I know for a fact that it's due to a condition known as neurogenic bladder, a common complication of spinal injuries. I've done my own reading and research. My bladder isn't receiving signals from my brain and urine is backing up into my kidneys causing my excruciating lower back and flank pain, destroying my kidneys, and taking decades off of my lifespan as they sit and do nothing.

They prescribed Flomax, as though my bladder problems are related to my prostate. They're not. I've tried to tell the prison healthcare staff what I believe my problems are to no avail. Dr. Baker (Jacksonville's finest quack) told me, "I don't base my diagnosis off of what you tell me your symptoms are. This is prison. Prisoners lie. I base my diagnosis off of test results, and your kidney function is fine." I recently read that kidney function can be normal with 80 percent of your kidneys destroyed.

Anyway, these are my problems, and I don't need to bore you with them. You probably have your own problems to deal with. Don't we all?

Walt was one of the first people transferred to Pittsfield. I would have been on the same bus sitting next to him if not for my medical hold. Walt's loss was a hard hit for the program to take. Chavez was also slated for transfer, but he had an educational hold because he was mere weeks away from earning his Associate's Degree. They had restarted limited school, allowing those who'd already been enrolled to finish out the semesters they'd begun prior to the quarantine. Hustle and Nelly scrambled to get their transfers squashed, talking to various influential staff with whom they held sway. Nelly was the facility law clerk and a certified paralegal, after all, and not easily replaced. Hustle was Hustle. They both believed (incorrectly) that they'd been successful in averting their transfers.

Ms. Briney was disheartened by these events. She had been facing ever-growing criticism and derision from Van Winkle and Delaney for Level Up. At one of their meetings Briney inquired about moving Level Up into phase two where participants could attend classes that offered sentence credits (time off of their sentences).

"That's not going to happen," said Van Winkle.

"Why not? It's what you agreed to and what we promised these guys back in the beginning," she replied.

"We're not doing it," he replied.

What he was saying through his actions, if not out loud, was, "Damn it, Briney, nobody thought this thing would last past the second week. The only reason it even happened is because Roberson was on board with it, but he's gone now. At first we thought it would be funny to just watch you crash and burn, but now you're turning into a real pain in the ass. You're taking participants away from GEO, and we can't have that."

Level Up was, in fact, taking participants away from GEO. Word had already gotten back to us that several of our ex-participants wanted to drop GEO and return to our program. They weren't feeling GEO and tried to make suggestions.

"The way they do groups in Level Up is they…"

"STOP TALKING ABOUT THAT DAMN LEVEL UP! WE'RE NOT LEVEL UP!" a counselor would snap in response.

At any rate, the sniping at Ms. Briney was continuous. Ms. Delaney filed a grievance with the union to have the social workers' job descriptions modified at Jacksonville in order to prohibit them from facilitating any of the life skills classes that they were specifically trained to do. Of course, the grievance was successful because Delaney was…well, you know.

It's not what you know, but who you…whatever. The job description was modified, making Jacksonville the only facility in the entire IDOC where social workers don't teach life skills classes. Ms. Briney's new job description stated that her only function was to perform prisoner assessments.

Prisoners in the program picked up on what was happening.

"Man, they be treating Ms. Briney. They really did that to that lady, they're about to shut her program down."

"This ain't her program, stupid, it's our program. She gets paid the same whether she does this or not, she was doing it for us. We're the ones who are getting treated."

Ms. Briney had had enough. She was ready to leave and confided in a select few of us that she would be putting in her two-week notice soon. No one could blame her. She had striven to go above and beyond, had exceeded everyone's expectations and then, as a result of her success, was shunned and sabotaged by her coworkers and superiors. What she had worked so hard to build and develop they eagerly sought to destroy. It wasn't a healthy work environment, and we didn't blame her for leaving.

Nelly, Hustle, Ty, Dolla, and Shakur were the next to learn that they were on the transfer bus. The C/Os came and told them to pack their property, they were leaving for Pittsfield Work Camp. Both Nelly and Hustle had believed they'd successfully thwarted their transfers, but whatever arrangements had been made, Van Winkle had clearly overridden.

Now Walt, Nelly, Hustle, Dolla, Ty, Shakur, and DeBerry were all gone, each of them irreplaceable in their own ways as mentors. Chavez, Unstable Able, and myself were the last men standing. Cole and Cody threw in the towel immediately, calling it quits. They didn't leave the wing, just stopped conducting their groups. The remaining mentors kept groups going as best we could with the help of two participants, Larry Betts and Bobby James, stepping up as acting mentors.

Try as we did, the knockout blow came when they filled our entire program wing up to full capacity with nonparticipants. You won't believe this; they sent us the nasty, thirsty, thieving coots from the old man deck in Housing Unit 5. It was like a nightmare. I'd wanted so badly to get away from them, and now here I was back among them, drowning in them. Rapists and tree jumpers and pedophiles, oh my. The day they moved onto our wing I overheard two of the nasty geezers talking as they were getting into the shower.

"Goddamn, man, look how clean these showers are!"

"Yeah man, I know! These motherfuckers over here must never get in the shower!"

We were once again 100 men strong, standing room only. The old men nastied up our clean wing in very short order. Hair and spit in the sinks. The smell of unwashed old man balls wafting up and down the hallways from the shower dodgers. Discarded soap pieces, soap boxes, and other debris in the showers from the ones who did take showers. Trash on the floor. The immediate theft of any item you left unattended for even a second. On the third day of their arrival one of them shit in the shower.

We did our best to stem the tide of filth, but the wing just felt grimy all of the time now. There were less than 350 prisoners left in Jacksonville, not even enough to fill up two housing units, but the administration had decided to consolidate us all into a single area. The only wing they left alone was the GED program wing.

Imagine that.

The administration had learned nothing from the pandemic. Two weeks after we'd been concentrated into one area an illness spread through our building like wildfire. Fortunately, it was only a summer cold, but all of us got sick. No one dared put in for sick call because none of us wanted to go back on quarantine.

Our wing underwent a massive change in vibe, radically different from what it had been. Luckily, we ended up with some decent guys in Room 10 (someone somewhere had been looking out for us), but still. Nelly's empty bunk was occupied by a meth-addled young man who everyone called Chokey. He looked like a cast member of the television show "Swamp People."

He was named Chokey because he had a nervous tic that caused him to place his hands around his neck and choke himself whenever he was uncomfortable. I couldn't help but wonder how that had played out in court. He's just one example. I could write 50 more.

That's what we were dealing with.

Here's Chokey. This is what we were dealing with.

The rag-tag remnant of mentors managed to limp to week eight in our new cycle (let's say) and we decided that we should pass out certificates early. Participants were allowed to miss two sessions and still graduate, so we'd technically met our minimum graduation requirements. In light of the uncertainty under which we lived, where any one of us might be transferred on any given day, we felt it would be best. It would have been a shame for the participants to have put in all that work, weeks worth, and been transferred without receiving a certificate.

Cody, Chavez, and myself went to the academic building to prepare the certificates with Ms. Briney. This was a process that normally took three or four days, but we speed-balled it and knocked it out in one day. Teamwork makes the dream work.

It was an involved task that entailed much more than simply slapping names onto certificates. The corresponding information had to be logged into Ms. Briney's files so she could enter the data into the computer and ensure that the certificates of completion for each group were recorded in each prisoner's master file in the computer program CHAMPS. Despite our haste, we amazingly got every single certificate correct except for four of them; all four of Cole's, our fellow mentor. Even though Cole and Cody had quit, we'd let them get their certificates, as well.

Cole's given name was Stuart Coleman. Somehow, Chavez had spelled it a different way on each certificate. He was Stewert Coleman, and then Stewart Colman, and yet again he was Stuewart Colemen. Last, but definitely not least (and I have no idea how Chavez did this one), he was Stewart Colemart.

0 for 4, Chavez. Great job.

It was an easy fix, but Cole got all bent out of shape about it, completely overreacting. He came up to Chavez and I.

"Whose certificates are these?"

"Yours," Chavez replied.

"I don't know whose they are, but they aren't mine! Look at the name on this I.D. and look at these certificates. Ain't one of them the same name. How do you do that? How's that happen?"

"Take it easy, Colemart," said Chavez. "It's not a big deal. We'll get you straightened out tomorrow."

Cole believed that Chavez had did it on purpose, but he didn't. Chavez was just messed up like that. The next day Colemart got his certificates with his name spelled correctly on each one. No harm, no foul.

The day came when Ms. Briney left. It was a bummer, but she was moving on to bigger and better things. The program was seemingly over at last. I was ready to let it die when two separate conversations changed my mind.

First, a participant approached me one day out of the blue. I won't put his name out there because of confidentiality (what's said in group, stays in group) but I'll tell you he was a participant in the parenting skills class I had facilitated.

"Hey, Nicky," he said. "I know they shot this program down, but I just wanted to say thanks, man."

"For what? I asked.

"That dad survey that you gave us in parenting class, man. I hadn't been talking to her for a minute. She's 12, but I sent her that survey and she wrote back and now she's on my email and we're rotating on the regular and…just thanks, bro. For real."

"No problem, bro. I'm glad to hear it."

For parenting class I'd typed up these dad surveys, basically questionnaires about your child's interests and lives. I got the idea from another parenting class I'd taken in Danville. I'd had copies made and handed them out to the class participants.

It was easy to fall into a pattern and go through the motions when facilitating groups. Sometimes you just don't think about the results that might happen. It's ironic that I would be facilitating a parenting class, I know, looking at my track record as a father. Dismal. But our group had made a real difference in this person's life. What other differences had we made? What differences could we make in the future?

After this I was approached by a participant named Dank. One thing I have to say about Dank, he was even bigger than Nelly. Dank was bench pressing over 500 pounds. There ain't a whole lot of people on planet earth who can do that, especially after a year of quarantine and no working out. That's Olympic ballpark numbers.

Dank expressed his opinion that Level Up had been too good of a concept to let simply fade into oblivion. Why should we allow them to win? He felt we should try to keep it going, and I agreed.

As it turned out, the reason they'd consolidated all the prisoners was because they were renovating all of the housing units. Plumbing, shower tiles, floors, painting, the works. When the renovations were complete in all housing units, everyone would return to their original places. Or at least that was the rumor.

Time to make some moves.

First, I spoke to the facility's other social worker, Ms. Stucka. She agreed to oversee the program, though she admitted that she wouldn't be as nearly hands-on as Ms. Briney had been. Another pro Level Up prisoner who had juice within the institution also spoke with her, a guy named Wood. Dank spoke to her as well. We even tried to talk to Ms. Delaney to get her on board, playing to her need to be in charge, but she all but told us to get the hell out of her face talking about Level Up. Oh well. Can't blame a guy for trying.

My second move was more of a gamble. I didn't know how this person was going to react.

It was Lieutenant Dodds.

I approached him and outlined my intentions to keep the program alive. Much to my surprise he was 100 percent on board. He told me to bring the list of participants directly to him when renovations were over and we were ready to restart. He also said to keep the list down to 50 or less in order to ensure that all the participants got bottom bunks, and he assured me that he would personally make sure that no nonparticipants were moved onto our wing.

Well, all right then.

I guess Level Up wasn't going out like no punk after all.

Epilogue

Pandemic Overtime

We're all in this weird place now. Is the pandemic over? Will things ever completely return to normal? Jacksonville hovers in this area of having one foot in normalcy and one foot in the pandemic. It's the difference between Pepsi and Diet Pepsi. Pepsi was pre-pandemic. Post-pandemic is Diet Pepsi. It's like if you haven't had Pepsi in a year-and-a-half and someone gives you a diet one.

"This tastes sort of like Pepsi, but it's off somehow. It doesn't taste quite the same as I remember it."

COVID brought a storm of changes to the IDOC. Our prisoner count has never been lower during the entire 22 years I've been in prison. They've switched over to an incentive-based corrections model. It's what officers call Hug-A-Thug.

Jacksonville is now slated to become a reentry center, like Kewannee or Murphysboro. Reentry centers are a relatively new concept within the IDOC. It's a facility that endeavors to prepare its prisoners for release as opposed to forcefully regimenting every aspect of their daily routines. There is no line movement in a reentry center. Feel hungry? Walk out and go to the chow hall when you feel like it. Need something from the store that you're out of? Walk out of your housing unit and go to the commissary whenever you feel like going. Want to work out? Go to the yard. Total unrestricted free movement within the institution's gates.

It's as free as you can be while still being in prison. This freedom comes at a price, however. You must be committed to participating in multiple life skills classes and rehabilitation programs, not unlike Level Up.

Many of the staff here are adamantly against the reentry concept. They are fighting it.

"I won't do it! I'll quit! What are we now, camp cupcake?"

Many of them are definitely not on board with the agenda. As I type these words I sit in Housing Unit 5 waiting for the renovations on the Level Up wing to be completed so I can get the hell away from this God forsaken old man deck. Level Up 2.0 will reboot with a new cast of characters.

There are rumors that none of us will be in Jacksonville much longer, that they want to start out their reentry phase with a new batch of prisoners. But you can't live your life on what might happen, so I'm planning on Level Up.

Jacksonville looks much better today than it did on the day I arrived, but there's still a shabbiness to it. Asphalt sidewalks. Fresh paint on the walls with splatter marks all over the baseboards, electrical outlets and light switches. It glistens like a well-polished, old, worn-out shoe.

I don't know what the future may bring, but I know that my fight continues. Many fights on many fronts. My fight against Wexford. My fight for clemency. My fight to walk the straight and narrow path. My fight to regain my health.

We all have our struggles, our own unique hardships, our own fights. I'll do mybest in my many fights.

Good luck to all of you in yours.

AFTERWORD

This is what we went through in the pandemic, and it may not be over. Even now, as of this writing, the delta variant is raging among the unvaccinated. Two prisons I know of are currently back on full lockdown quarantine.

In this endeavor, I took on a responsibility for the well being of others, much the same as a bus driver or airline pilot. The way in which they're responsible for the safety of their passengers, I felt the same weight of responsibility in the telling of this story on behalf of those without means or ability to do so themselves. I hope I have not let them down.

I hope I have delivered them safely to their destinations.

Those who have sent their photographs to my publisher for placement within these pages, without ever first having seen a single word I've written, placed in me a degree of trust I would never have dreamed of betraying. I am sure there were things I forgot, of which remain unwritten, and I probably didn't do as good a job relating the bleak and hopeless desperation of quarantine as I should have.

I may have missed the mark for which I have aimed, but I want all of those for whom this book is written- prisoners in general, prisoners in the IDOC more specifically, and the prisoners of Jacksonville Correctional Center, especially those six who died from COVID, most of all- to know that I did my best. I worked harder on this than I've ever worked on anything in my entire life, writing and rewriting time and again to get the words just right and tell it as it was. This is as good as I can do. I have nothing left in the tank. I left it all on the court.

I don't care who in authority this book may irk, anger, or annoy. Fuck them. My only concern is that I didn't disappoint those whom this book is about. It's okay if I never win a Pulitzer. I probably won't. This doesn't have to be the greatest piece of literature ever created, I just want the people I wrote it for to be happy with it,

And I also hope it doesn't suck.

ACKNOWLEDGEMENTS

First and foremost, thanks to God. Second, thanks to Cathy Chittick for giving me my life. Thanks to Carl Chittick for giving me music and a work ethic. Thanks to Frank Reuter and everyone at Cadmus Publishing. Thanks to my brother, Walter Edwards. Thanks to Walter's girl, Shamekia Branch. Special thanks to my brothers Joseph King, Arnell Williams, and Joshua Chavez. Thanks to all the mentors and participants of the Level Up program. Thanks to Rochelle Briney.

Special thanks to my sister, Jenny DaCosta. And thank you Ms. Sumpter. Thanks to Jesus Camacho and the Camacho family.

During my decades of incarceration, I have met thousands of people. A select few made me a better person for having known them, and although they may not have had a direct influence on this book, without them it may not have been written. Thanks to Oscar "Lil Man" Martinez for showing a scared, twenty-something neutron white boy how to move in jail and prison.

"Don't be a snitch, don't be a bitch, and you'll be fine", he said to me in Cook County Jail more than 21 years ago. Great advice.

Thanks to Cedric Bouchee, who made me a better musician. Thank you, Marco Becerra, a true friend who has the strongest work ethic and more heart than anyone I've ever known. Thank you, Chaplains Manny Rojas and Daniel Shreve, for making me stronger in Christ. Still a work in progress. Thank you, my fellow military veterans Gary Swafford, John Burton, and Art Garrison for being friends at a time in my life when I needed friends most. Thanks to Counselors Joseph Smith, Melissa Robbins, Felecia Adkins, Scotty Moore and Jamie Tate for treating me like a human being instead of a prisoner. Thanks to Chad Tranchant and Dakota Getz for the same reason. If I forgot anyone, I apologize.

I guess you must not be that important.

ABOUT THE AUTHOR

Nicholas Chittick is a writer, musician and jailhouse lawyer. He currently resides in Illinois against his will.

ABOUT THE ILLUSTRATOR

Jesus Camacho is a thirty-year old man who lives on the south side of Rockford, Illinios. He is a resident of the United States, who's family immigrated from San Jose Agua Azul, Guanajuato, Mexico. He is a dedicated father, brother, and son.

CPSIA information can be obtained
at www.ICGtesting.com
Printed in the USA
BVHW040525230222
629775BV00011B/900

9 781637 511305